# Start Thinking

# Start Thinking

Daily starters to inspire thinking in primary classrooms

**Marcelo Staricoff and Alan Rees**

Imaginative Minds, Leonard House, 321 Bradford Street, Digbeth, Birmingham B5 6ET

**For Emily and Thomas (M.S.)**
**For Jessica (A.R.)**

Published in 2005
By Imaginative Minds Ltd
1st Floor, Leonard House
321 Bradford Street, Birmingham B5 6ET


ISBN: 1-90480-602-3

## Acknowledgements

The authors would like to thank the children, staff, governors and parents at Westbury Park Primary School for their active interest, their enthusiastic responses and their good wishes.

We are grateful to Ruth Deakin-Crick, Deborah Eyre, Robert Fisher, Fen Marshall, Roger Sutcliffe, Lynne McClure, Helen Wilson, James Nottingham, Barry Hymer and Steve Williams for their encouragement and support. Also to Gustavo Staricoff who inspired many of the mathematical starters, Anna Staricoff, Rosalia and Carlos Staricoff, and Sian Rees who all gave invaluable support throughout the whole process.

Members of the Bristol Schools Thinking Skills Group also deserve credit for providing a stimulating forum where ideas and thoughts could be shared. Therefore, we thank:

- Helen Heap, Beccy Blight, Tess Christy and Judith Davies (Ashley Down Infants School)
- Tony Tween, John Clark and Catherine Turl (Christ Church C of E Primary School)
- Lynda Heayberd and Leah Tomlin (Colston's Primary School)
- Clare Clohessy (Elmlea Infant School)
- Lynne Pye (Henleaze Infant School)
- Maggie Cosgrove (Henleaze Junior School)
- Toni Glazzard, Ginny Perrin and Katie Watson (Hotwells Primary School)
- Karen Clark and Kate Murray (Oldbury Court Primary School)
- Marion Derham (St George C of E Primary School)
- Cat Norrie (South Street Primary School)
- Pam Cowley and Mike Gregg (Stoke Bishop C of E Primary School)
- Eleni Charalambous and Kate Humphreys (Westbury Park Primary School)
- Sonia Goddard and Joe Tett (Weston Park Primary School)
- Jenny Brookes (Primary Gifted and Talented Consultant)

# Start Thinking

# Thinking Skills Starters



*Thinking Skills Starters* are enjoyable, open-ended challenges that are suitable for all pupils. They are straightforward yet demanding when used in the right way. We use the term *Starter* to describe a task that greets children as they first enter the classroom in the morning. They start to tackle it as their teacher takes the register. After 10 minutes the teacher and pupils share the ideas the pupils have come up with. They discuss possible implications and extensions of those ideas. Then they move onto other things. Pupils have the option of continuing to work on *Starters* in their own time.

Although this remains the preferred model for most teachers who have used the *Thinking Skills Starters*, some prefer to use them at other times: just before break or lunch, first thing in the afternoon or whenever an appropriate opportunity arises in lessons. The aim of a *Starter* is to challenge and entertain children by drawing on their own experiences, memories and resources. *Starters* are designed to be accessible to all, regardless of ability, gender, age and sometimes even language. *Starters* provide children and teachers with the freedom to experiment with their thinking and exploit their creativity – and all this without the fear of being judged right or wrong or of feeling pressurised to finish a *Starter* in a certain amount of time. Very often children continue working on their *Starters* at other times and with other people: during school or at home, by themselves, with friends or with their families. So, for example, the *Four Fours Challenge* (page 23), where the numbers 1 to 20 are derived using four fours each time, inspired a group of four children to meet up after school and work out every number up to 150! They at once became celebrities throughout the school .

Unlike other kinds of work at school, *Starters* are not marked or checked; the children only share what they have done if they wish to. In our school, *Starters* are providing children, teachers and parents with bucketfuls of fun and some very interesting routes to thinking about the world around them – anything and everything could be turned into a *Starter* if viewed and presented in the right way.

The benefits we have observed in our school after using *Starters* regularly is the driving force behind this book. Through *Starters*, children have enlightened our days on so many occasions through their originality, their sense of humour and their talents – some of which we never dreamed they possessed. What encouraged us even more to compile the book were the numerous comments from teachers, children and parents who, having had a taste of *Thinking Skills Starters*, became thoroughly and irreversibly addicted. The positive impact of *Starters* is due, we believe, to the ease with which they can be implemented and managed, coupled with the almost immediate intellectual and emotional rewards for children and teachers.

## Benefits of Thinking Skills Starters

*They make me feel revved up for the day. I want to skip time to get to the next one. We are allowed to bring our own ones in!* (Ollie). *They can never stop. They get right into my brain! [Ben]. They have a really good influence on your thinking* (Charlie)

Having begun every day for the past two or three years with a *Thinking Skills Starter*, I believe that they provide a very useful means through which a teacher can get to know what motivates individual children. The daily *Starter* is a valuable tool to help me improve my relationships with those children I teach. *Starters* are very flexible – they can be used as stand-alone activities such as listing 'what makes you laugh' or they can be woven into the subject-based curriculum. For example, as a precursor to tackling topics on *Ourselves* or *Healthy Living* in Science, children try to think of differences and similarities between blood and ketchup (page 61). The task is fun to do and the ideas generated by the children can be used to guide and structure the way the topic is taught from then on. *Starters* often give teachers an insight into pupils' current levels of understanding, their misconceptions and topics that they may be interested in researching further.

Teachers have offered various reasons to explain why children enjoy *Starters* so much. One of the most important factors, we think, is that the children do not perceive them as 'school work'. They feel that they are being allowed to have fun with their learning, even though they are at school. They are being given the opportunity to think without the anxiety of being judged and without being limited to pre-defined outcomes. *Starters* seem to create the conditions for learning that mirror the way very young children discover how the world functions – through play. The Foundation Stage of education provides a magnificent example of this approach to learning and we feel that *Starters* sustain their excitement for learning and discovery as the children progress through Key Stages One and Two.

When teachers use *Starters*, they can have a tremendous impact on children's self esteem. Within a relatively short space of time children are exposed to a wide range of challenges. Each child seems to discover a personal favourite with regular frequency. It is in the sharing of their thinking with the whole class that children are able to experience the wonderful feeling of having their ideas valued and respected in a supportive environment. They realise that they are contributing to the learning of their peers – and of the teacher as well.

## How to use Thinking Skills Starters

*They make me feel welcome and confident to create a new piece of knowledge. If I created a Mind Map of the Starters, it would be huge!* (Rhodri)

Hopefully you are now convinced of the value of *Starters* and have a feel for the kind of learning we hope they will stimulate. The next step is to discuss the best way to implement them in your own classroom.

My personal preference, as a Key Stage 2 teacher, is to indulge the class with a *Thinking Skills Starter* on a daily basis. The beginning of the day is always a very special time as it sets the pace for what is to come. If you start the day with a *Thinking Skills Starter*, the classroom acquires a very peaceful, welcoming and purposeful atmosphere in which it is a joy to take the register and to observe the way children are dedicated to tackling the current challenge.

As the children enter the classroom in the morning, they are greeted by classical music and a *Starter* written up on the board. As the *Starters* are self explanatory, the children go to their seats and begin to tackle the task in *Thinking Skills Exercise Books* which are solely dedicated to *Starters*. These books are very special to the children. They are the only books that are never marked or even looked at by myself or anyone else. This seems to free the children from fear of judgement and encourages them to experiment with their thinking, to take risks and have a go. In the meantime I take the register and when that is done, we devote time to sharing the outcomes of their thinking on the current *Starter* and we discuss possible implications and extensions of their ideas.

So, for example, if the starter is to list countries they know, I might ask them to think of as many different kinds of categories as they can with which to group the countries. The children may come up with suggestions like 'hemispheres', 'continents', hot and cold', 'dangerous and safe' or 'places I would like to go for my holiday'. The ten minutes or so often produce my favourite moments of the day. The children's thoughts can be so original, so inspirational, so them. This sharing time and the playing with ideas through processes such as categorising and prioritising as well as the deepening of thinking though processes such as giving reasons and assessing alternatives is what makes using the *Starters* useful for developing pupils thinking skills. I encourage risk taking thought the sharing of tentative thoughts and I don't insist that only children who finish the whole task can share their work.

### After Thinking Skills Starters

The whole cycle of introducing a *Starter*, sharing and discussing takes no more than 20 minutes and it leaves the class buzzing with excitement and gripped by positive attitudes to thinking and learning which set us up wonderfully for the day ahead. Through *Starters* we are creating a classroom culture in which we all learn together rather than one where only teachers teach and only children learn.

Although not every *Starter* will interest every child in the class, most *Starters* will help children to develop their critical curiosity and their eagerness to come up with interesting answers or solutions. The varied nature of *Starters* means that the interests of every child will connect regularly with a daily *Starter*. When this happens, *Starters* often stimulate bouts of extended research and problem solving. The open-ended nature of starters encourages this urge to independent work; students are further motivated by the idea of sharing their achievements with the rest of the class. We encourage children to persevere with those *Starters* that grip their interest and to work on them outside lesson times with friends and relatives. We also encourage them follow their interests and ideas where they lead. If a *Starter* becomes a bridge to other projects then fine, we look forward to children sharing their new discoveries with us. We make time for children to share their extended work on previous *Starters* whenever they are ready to do to so. I have written a detailed account of how one *Starter* stimulated an impressive mathematical investigation (See appendix Two).

### Starters with all age groups

*Starters* can be enjoyed by all children in the school. The emphasis on enjoyment and sharing is paramount so using *Starters* has to be carefully planned with the children's current abilities and routines in mind.

For example, Foundation and Year 1 teachers tend to work through *Starters* verbally, as a whole-class activity on the carpet and with the teacher recording children's thoughts. Year 2 and 3 children may start to use *Thinking Skills Exercise Books*, but may choose not do *Starters* every day. Instead they may save them as 'special treats', to be done once or twice a week. It is so important that the children look forward to *Starters* and never regard them as a chore or as 'more work'. Equally, the teacher may wish to use them at times other than the beginning of the day, or they may form the basis of homework tasks or even as open-ended challenges for children to work together with younger partners.

*The visual starters are perfect for young children – fun, creative and non-threatening* (Eleni Charalambous and Vicky Duggan, Year 1 Teachers)

This versatile nature of the *Starters* is one of their most appealing features and it is important that teachers feel they have a completely free reign to implement them in ways that are most appropriate to their particular group of children.

### Starters and 'Habits of Mind'

*Starters* can play their part in encouraging children to develop dispositions or Habits of Mind that are positive for learning. There is a growing literature on this topic and an increasing awareness that positive dispositions are important factors contributing a child's progress in school. Using *Starters* will help you to highlight and develop dispositions such as: being resilient, thinking flexibly, finding humour, taking risks, communicating with clarity, problem posing, using imagination and being methodical.

A first step to developing these kinds of dispositions is to draw children's attention to them when you set a *Starter* or when children share their ideas. For example, you could say that a certain *Starter* requires them to work flexibly, carefully or persistently. You could praise children's efforts when they bring one of the dispositions to bear on their work – particularly when they commit themselves to one or more of the thinking processes listed with the *Starter* (for independent and regular commitment to processes such as imagining, evaluating alternatives and giving reasons is evidence of the development of positive learning dispositions). If you are trying to promote a particular disposition with your pupils, the *Starters* will provide you with examples to draw on. You could say: 'remember when Charlie took home the *Four Fours Starter* and worked on it for weeks. That took persistence didn't it. Was it worth it Charlie?' You could easily draw the children's attention to a time when one of them came up with something no-one else had thought of, showing evidence of the disposition to think flexibly. *Starters* can help you to develop positive dispositions in your classroom.

### The impact of Thinking Skills Starters

*They wind me up like a clockwork mouse so I buzz through the rest of the day* (Nicola)

*Starters* have had a fantastic impact on the school as a whole. In the mornings the teachers often meet in the corridor to discuss who's doing which *Starter* and to compare notes on how they were received by children. Trying the same *Starter* with different year groups and then getting the children together to share their thinking can be a fascinating exercise! Some schools are even using them as warm ups for the staff before staff meetings and INSET days.

The impact that *Starters* have had among children, teachers, parents and governors has been, and continues to be, incalculable. What started as a bit of fun in the mornings has become one of the main driving forces behind the concept of a whole-school thinking-skills approach to the Curriculum, and of the way the children have become increasingly motivated to be active participants in their own learning. Alan Rees, the Headteacher of Westbuty Park School, has written an appendix to this book explaining how *Starters* fit into the bigger picture of developing creative teaching and learning and thinking skills across the curriculum. Have fun!

### Chapter Structure and Organisation

The book is divided into six chapters, each one dealing with a different genre of *Starter*. The final chapter consists of 'extras' that don't fit easily in the other chapters but have proved successful with children. Chapters are designed so that the level of challenge increases as the chapters progress. We don't want to exclude any teacher from having a go or adapting any of the *Starters* to suit the particular needs and abilities of the children they teach. The gradual progression within each chapter gives some order and structure for teachers trying to decide which ones to do.

As already mentioned, the *Starters* can be used to introduce, support or extend work in the curriculum – each *Starter* contains a 'comments' section which may contain any or all of the following:

- potential links to particular curriculum areas and topics
- useful experiences from teachers who have used it before
- appropriate times to use it
- ideas to extend the activity to deepen thinking such as giving reasons, categorising ideas or identifying similarities and differences.

I'm sure you will find plenty more connections and applications than are mentioned in the book. At the foot of each *Starter* there are two lists, one that records curriculum content that the *Starter* may connect to and one that suggests thinking processes that the *Starter* will stimulate. The list of processes will also give you some ideas about how you might deepen thinking around each activity. So, for example, if the list includes 'giving reasons' then, during sharing time, you should ask children to give reasons for the choices they have made in the *Starter.* A complete index of content topics is included at the end of this book.

*They are really challenging and they give me a lot of confidence for my work. They stretch your brain in all sorts of ways and make you feel good about what you've done* (Jasmine). *When I get my book out, I try to think things that are in my imagination* (Simon)

Every *Starter* included in this book is someone's favourite – and we decided to accompany each one with at least one short worked example from a child who really enjoyed it. We have sometimes given examples of the work of more than one child to show a range of different kinds of responses or work from children of different ages. We have indicated what year children are in but haven't given each child's name. We have also corrected some of the children's spellings. For these *Starters*, it is the children's ideas that are most important and we wanted these to be shown as clearly as possible.

Very often a *Starter* will stimulate children to develop it further in their own way or even to turn it into a substantial on-going projects.

**Starters and thinking processes**

Different kinds of *Starters* stimulate different combinations of thinking processes. To tackle the mathematical *Starters*, for example, children often have to *devise methods, experiment and check.* Creative *Starters* require *invention, imagination* and often *visualisation.* Philosophical *Starters* stimulate the children to *value, question* and *interpret* while linguistic *Starters* prompt children to *experiment* with words and *assess alternatives*. All kinds of *Starters* provide plenty of opportunities for children to *give reasons, compare* similarities and differences and *classify*. You should grasp opportunities to develop these processes whenever possible during sharing time because they are building blocks for effective thinking across the curriculum. We have listed some processes at the foot of every *Starter* to remind you of what is happening and what could happen when children work on it and then share their thoughts. There is no hierarchy to the list and it is not meant to be definitive. The key processes are given in the table below.

| | | |
|---|---|---|
| Devising methods | Experimenting and checking | Interpreting |
| Prioritising | Ordering | Valuing |
| Assessing alternatives | Making meaning | Connecting |
| Recognising patterns | Comparing | Classifying |
| Remembering | Giving reasons | Improvising |
| Speculating | Inventing | Questioning |
| Enquiring | Imagining consequences | Generalising |
| Imagining | Visualising | Devising rules |

**Summary of how to use Starters**

1. Write the *Starter* on the board for pupils to see as they enter the room.
2. Provide any explanations or examples you think the children will need.
3. Allow pupils about 15 minutes to gather their ideas for the *Starter* by writing or drawing in their thinking skills exercise books. Younger children may need to talk rather than write or draw.
4. Invite pupils to share their ideas on the *Starter* paying attention to key processes such as *giving reasons, devising methods* or *categorising.*
5. Encourage pupils to continue adding ideas to their Starter at home if they want to. Be prepared to provide some sharing time in future sessions if children return with developed ideas.

# Starter Page Layout

We have aimed to make the layout of the pages explaining the Starters as straightforward as possible by omitting any unnecessary text. The layout is explained below using a sample page.

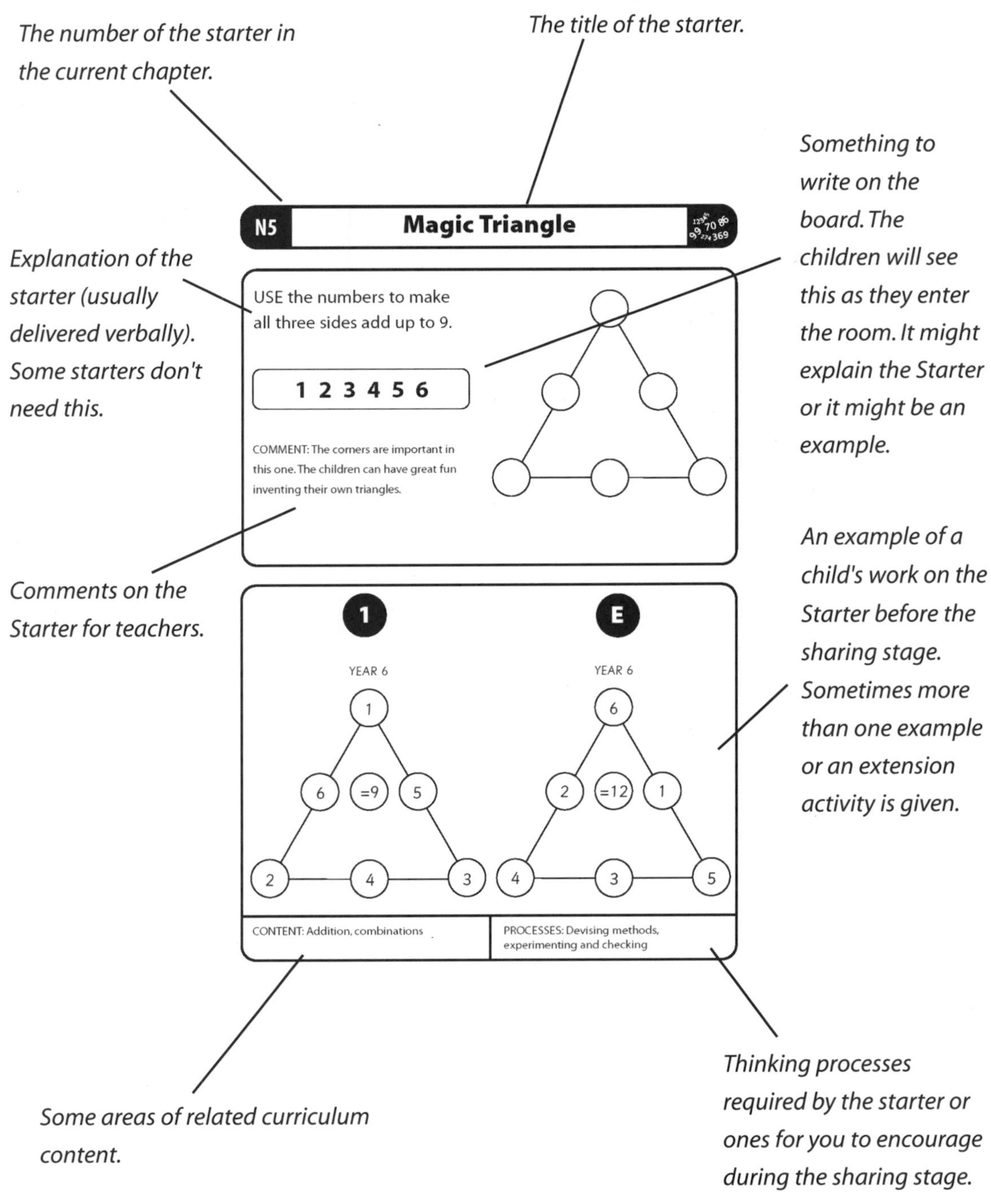

*The number of the starter in the current chapter.*
*The title of the starter.*
N5
Magic Triangle
*Something to write on the board. The children will see this as they enter the room. It might explain the Starter or it might be an example.*
*Explanation of the starter (usually delivered verbally). Some starters don't need this.*
USE the numbers to make all three sides add up to 9.
1 2 3 4 5 6
COMMENT: The corners are important in this one. The children can have great fun inventing their own triangles.
*Comments on the Starter for teachers.*
*An example of a child's work on the Starter before the sharing stage. Sometimes more than one example or an extension activity is given.*
1
E
YEAR 6
YEAR 6
1
6
=9
5
2
4
3
6
2
=12
1
4
3
5
CONTENT: Addition, combinations
PROCESSES: Devising methods, experimenting and checking
*Some areas of related curriculum content.*
*Thinking processes required by the starter or ones for you to encourage during the sharing stage.*

# Number Starters

N1

# Philosophical Numbers

## What is the biggest number you know?

COMMENT: This is particularly good as a discussion topic with younger children. Discussing the concept of infinity is so facinating. Can you ever get there? Does it exist? What is it? You could introduce negative numbers too. The concept that numbers go on for ever is quite awe inspiring!

1

YEAR 1

A million 1,000,000

A billion 1,000,000,000

A trillion 1,000,000,000,000

Infinity

Infinity is not a number!

CONTENT: Place value, infinity

PROCESSES: Remembering, speculating, imagining

N2

# Questions, Questions

## 6 is the answer. What are the questions?

COMMENT: Obviously you could choose any number. Encourage the children to think beyond obvious answers involving calculations. The ideas generated can be so original!

**1**

YEAR 2

The answer is ten.

3+7 =10

12-2 =10

5+5 =10

4+6 =10

800-600-100-50-40 =10

2+2+2+8 =10

**2**

YEAR 5

The answer is six.

3+3 4+2 5+1 6+0 2+4 1+5 0+6

What is half of twelve?

What is a quarter of twenty-four?

How old was my sister a year and a half ago?

How many sides does a hexagon have?

How many letters are there in my first name?

What year will I be in next year?

CONTENT: Place value, operations, checks

PROCESSES: Questioning, making meaning, connecting, inventing, speculating

# N3 Magic Square I

USE the numbers to make each row, column and diagonal add up to 6.

**1 1 1 2 2 2 3 3 3**

COMMENT: A lovely introduction to magic squares. Some children may not wish to attempt the diagonals to begin with, but encourage them to try, perhaps as an extension activity.

**1**

YEAR 3

| | | |
|---|---|---|
| 2 | 1 | 3 |
| 3 | 2 | 1 |
| 1 | 3 | 2 |

CONTENT: Addition, combinations

PROCESSES: Devising methods, experimenting and checking

# N4 Magic Square II

USE the numbers to make each row, column and diagonal add up to 15.

|   |   |   |
|---|---|---|
|   |   |   |
|   |   |   |
|   |   |   |

**1 2 3 4 5 6 7 8 9**

COMMENT: The key to this one is the middle number! Some children may not wish to attempt the diagonals to begin with as in N3.

**1**

YEAR 5

|   |   |   |
|---|---|---|
| 2 | 7 | 6 |
| 9 | 5 | 1 |
| 4 | 3 | 8 |

CONTENT: Addition, combinations

PROCESSES: Devising methods, experimenting and checking

N5

# Magic Triangle

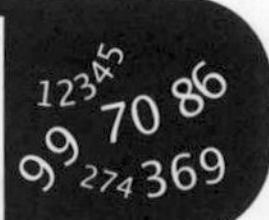


USE the numbers to make all three sides add up to 9.

**1 2 3 4 5 6**

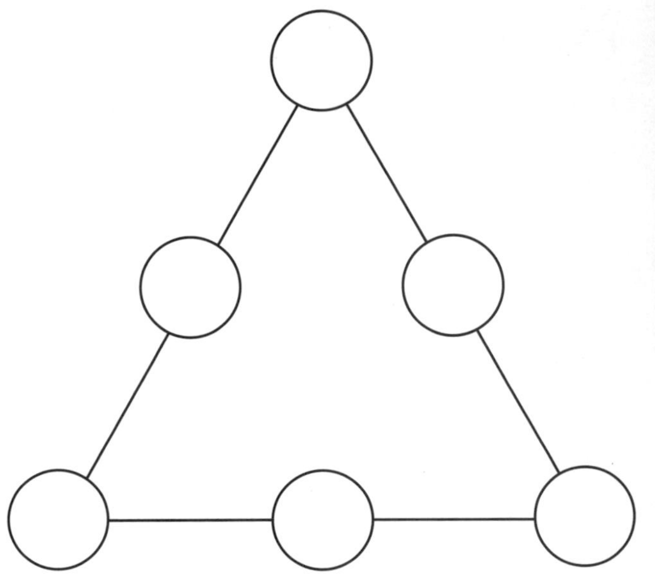

COMMENT: The corners are important in this one. The children can have great fun inventing their own triangles.

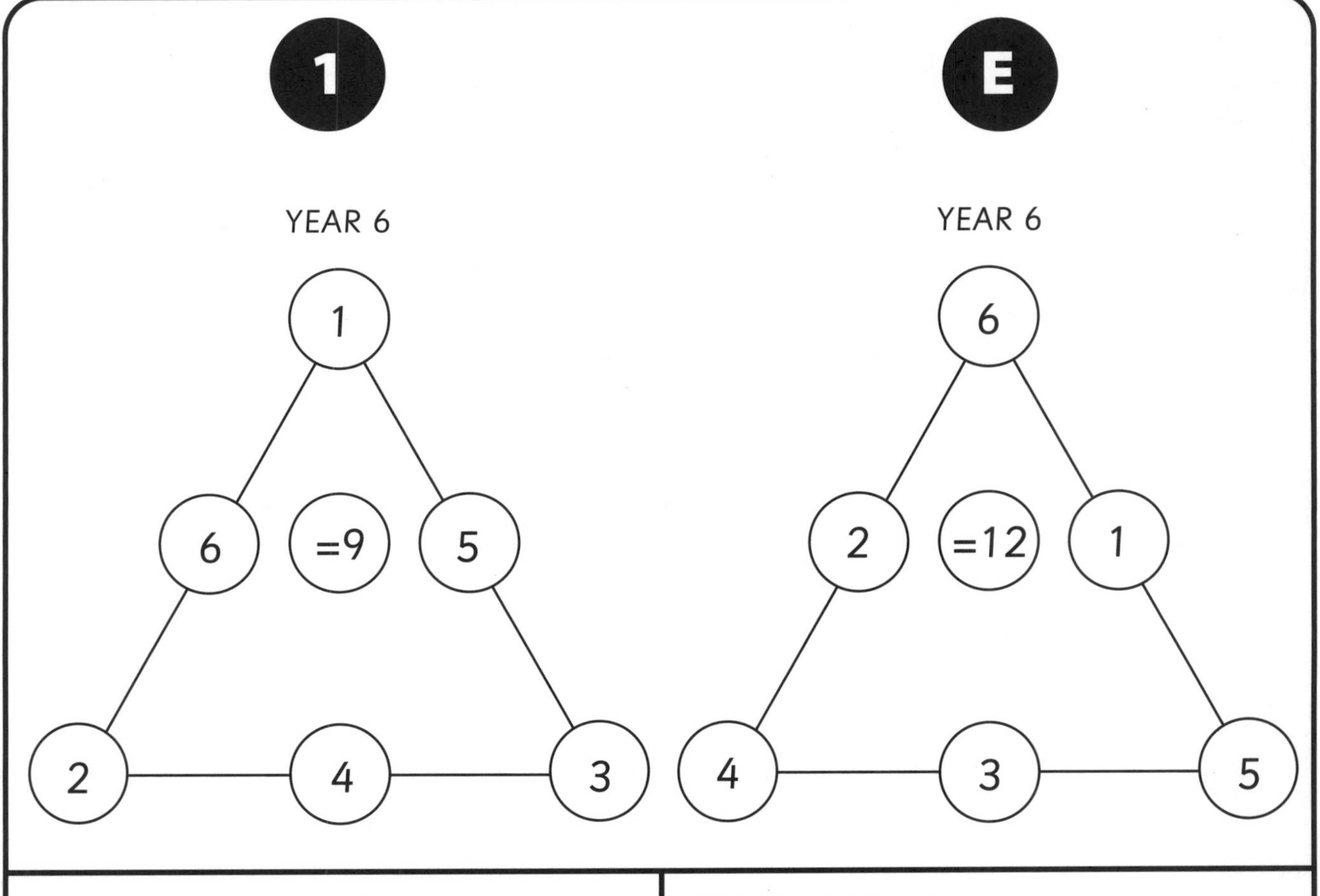


CONTENT: Addition, combinations

PROCESSES: Devising methods, experimenting and checking

# N6 Number Jigsaw

REARRANGE these numbers so there is one number between the two ones, two numbers between the two twos and three numbers between the two threes.

**1 1 2 2 3 3**

COMMENT: This challenge just requires a 'playing' approach. There is no mathematics involved. Once the children work it out, they will try to add two fours and then two fives, although the latter remains unsolved.

| 1 | E |
|---|---|
| YEAR 5<br>312132 | YEAR 5: *With four numbers between the two fours*<br>41312432 |
| CONTENT: Trial and error | PROCESSES: Devising methods, experimenting and checking, visualising |

N7

# Number Combinations

HOW MANY different 4-digit numbers can you make using the number in the box.

**1 9 6 5**

COMMENT: This challenge is enjoyable and is a very good introduction to the solving of problems by using a methodological approach – a step by step procedure that will guarantee the right answer.

**1**

YEAR 3

| | | |
|---|---|---|
| 1596 | 5619 | 6951 |
| 1569 | 5691 | 6915 |
| 1659 | 5916 | 9156 |
| 1695 | 5961 | 9165 |
| 1965 | 6159 | 9516 |
| 1956 | 6195 | 9561 |
| 5169 | 6519 | 9615 |
| 5196 | 6591 | 9651 |

CONTENT: Permutations

PROCESSES: Devising methods, experimenting and checking

# N8 Consecutive Numbers

USE consecutive numbers to make up numbers 1-20.

**1 + 2 = 3, 2 + 3 = 5, and so on...**

COMMENT: This challenge can be very easily adapted to suit age groups and abilities. Once children have achieved up to 20, there is no stopping them! It is interesting to note the numbers that cannot be made up in this way. Is there a pattern to them? What would be the next number after 16 that can't be made?

**1**

YEAR 5

| | |
|---|---|
| 1 = 0+1 | 11 = 5+6 |
| 2 = | 12 = 3+4+5 |
| 3 = 1+2 | 13 = 6+7 |
| 4 = | 14 = 2+3+4+5 |
| 5 = 2+3 | 15 = 1+2+3+4+5 |
| 6 = 1+2+3 | 16 = |
| 7 = 3+4 | 17 = 8+9 |
| 8 = | 18 = 3+4+5+6 |
| 9 = 2+3+4 | 19 = 9+10 |
| 10 = 1+2+3+4 | 20 = 2+3+4+5+6 |

CONTENT: Addition

PROCESSES: Devising methods, recognising patterns, experimenting and checking

# N9 Same Digit Numbers

GENERATE same-digit numbers by subtracting consecutive ones.

**654 – 321 = 333**
**876 – 543 = 333**

COMMENT: It's amazing how this happens and there are lots of different 'same numbers' that can be generated in this way. It's also interesting to see if the children can create same-digit-number answers of two digits or of more than three digits.

**1**

YEAR 5

654 – 321 = 333

765 – 432 = 333

876 – 543 = 333

**2**

YEAR 5

987 – 321 = 666

789 – 123 = 666

**E**

YEAR 5

9876 – 5432 = 4444

| CONTENT: Subtractions | PROCESSES: Devising methods, recognising patterns, experimenting and checking |
|---|---|

# N10 Summing Up

USE each number once
to make this sum correct.

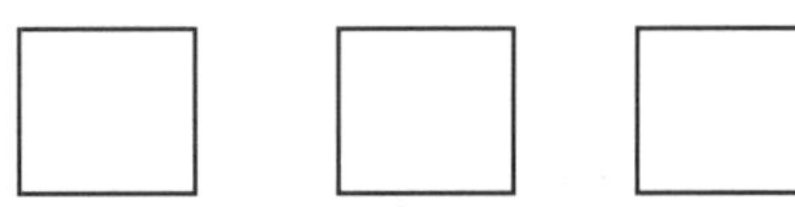

0 1 2 3 4 5 6 7 8 9

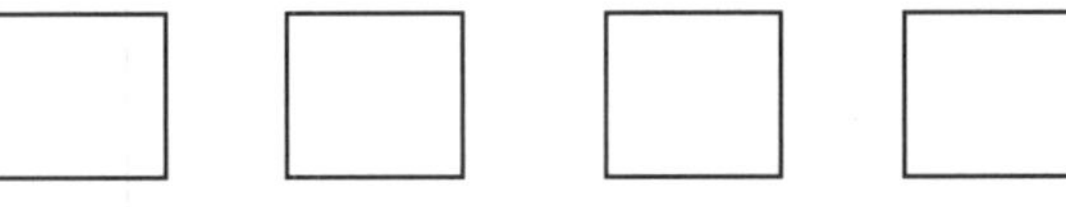

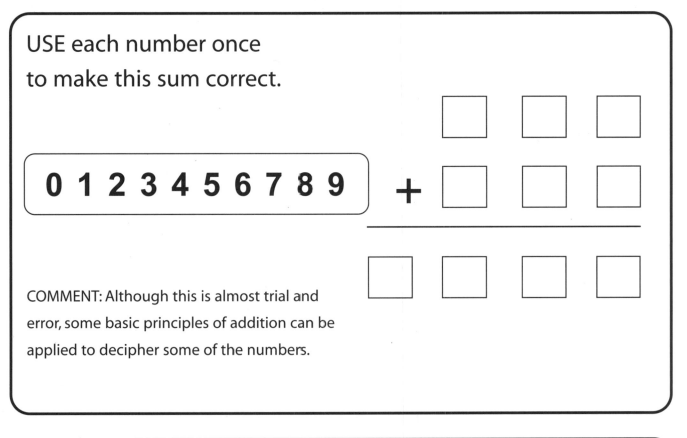

COMMENT: Although this is almost trial and error, some basic principles of addition can be applied to decipher some of the numbers.

**1**

YEAR 5

|   | 3 | 5 | 6 |
|---|---|---|---|
| + | 7 | 4 | 2 |
| 1 | 0 | 9 | 8 |

CONTENT: Addition, place value

PROCESSES: Devising methods, experimenting and checking

N11

# Parents and Children

INVESTIGATE what happens when you add up the six different two-digit numbers that can be generated from the number in the box.

**1 3 2**

COMMENT: This is why maths is so fascinating! Why should it be that patterns like these arise? It is interesting to see if children can find other three-digit numbers that behave in the same way.

**1**

YEAR 5

12 + 13 = 25

21 + 23 = 44

31 + 32 = 63

25 + 44 + 63 = <u>132</u>

**E**

YEAR 5: From <u>396</u>

96 + 93 = 189

69 + 63 = 132

39 + 36 = 75

189 + 132 + 75 = <u>396</u>

CONTENT: Addition, place value

PROCESSES: Devising methods, recognising patterns, experimenting and checking

# N12 Loop The Loop

WHAT IS the rule that generates the next number?

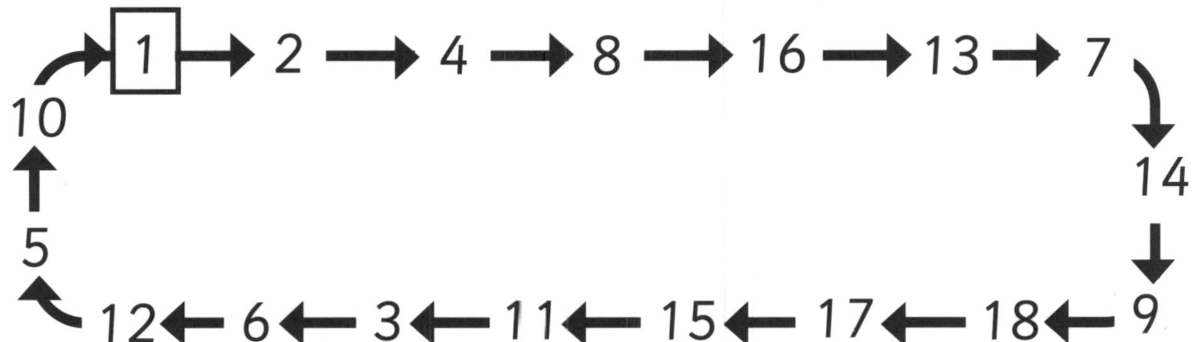

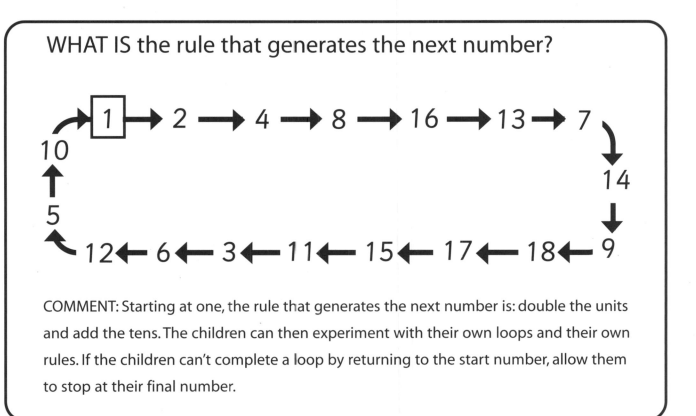

COMMENT: Starting at one, the rule that generates the next number is: double the units and add the tens. The children can then experiment with their own loops and their own rules. If the children can't complete a loop by returning to the start number, allow them to stop at their final number.

**1**

YEAR 5

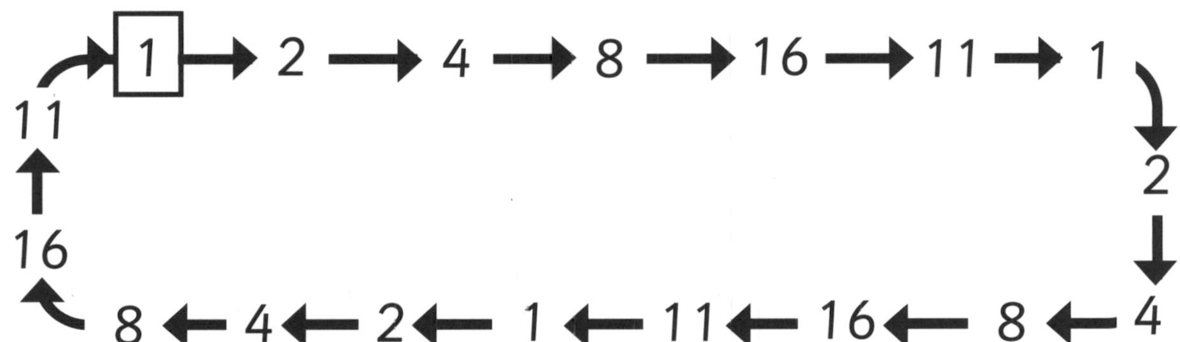

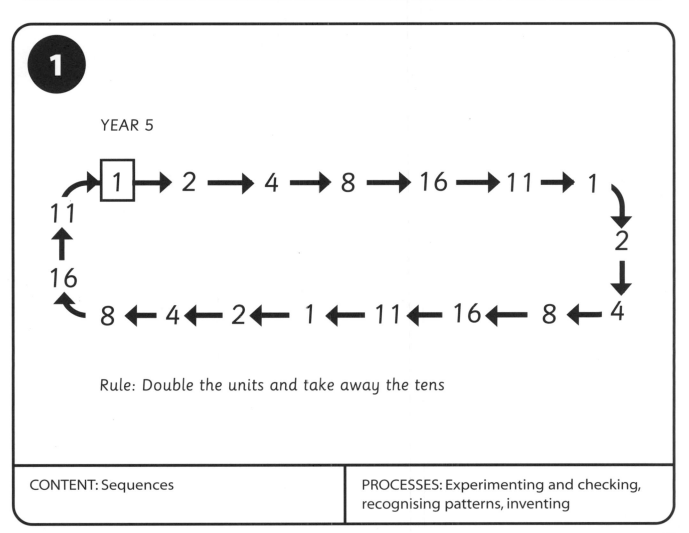

*Rule: Double the units and take away the tens*

| CONTENT: Sequences | PROCESSES: Experimenting and checking, recognising patterns, inventing |
|---|---|

# N13 One Day I'll Earn...

## Salary: £24,000 a year

How much is this per:

- month
- hour
- week
- minute
- day
- second

COMMENT: A wonderful way to practise multiplication and division, and to introduce children to concepts of worth and value. Go on to have the children look in the papers at salaries on offer and do the same calculations.

| 1 | E | E |
|---|---|---|
| YEAR 6<br>£24,000<br>£2,000 a month<br>£500 a week<br>£71.40 a day (7 days)<br>£3 per hour (24 hours)<br>5p per minute<br>0.08p per second | YEAR 6<br>£24,000<br>£2,000 a month<br>£500 a week<br>£100 a day(5 days)<br>£12.50 per hour (8 hours, 5 days)<br>21p per minute<br>0.4p per second | YEAR 6<br>£84,000<br>£7,000 a month<br>£1750 a week<br>£250 a day<br>£10.40 per hour 17p per minute<br>0.3p per second |

CONTENT: Problem solving, multiplication

PROCESSES: Devising methods, comparing, imagining consequences

## N14 Four Fours

USE FOUR 4s each time, and any operation, to make up numbers 1-20.

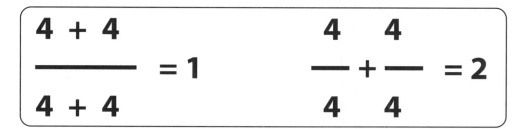

$$\frac{4+4}{4+4} = 1 \qquad \frac{4}{4} + \frac{4}{4} = 2$$

COMMENT: This will keep children amused for days and days! As you can see below there is no limit to how far one can go – up to 522 is the current record in our school. With the higher numbers it is useful to introduce to the children the concept of 4 squared, 4 cubed, 4! (Factorial i.e. 4x3x2x1) and 4 to the power of 0 which equals one. Enjoy!

**E**

YEAR 5

$1 = \frac{4+4}{4+4}$

$2 = 4^2 - 4^2 + 4^0 + 4^0$

$3 = \sqrt{4} + 4^0 + 4 - 4$

$4 = 4^2 - 4 - 4 - 4$

$5 = 4 + 4^0 - 4^0 + 4^0$

$6 = 4 + 4 - 4^0 - 4^0$

$7 = 4^2 - 4 - 4 - 4^0$

$8 = 4 + 4 + 4 - 4$

$9 = 4^2 - 4 - 4 + 4^0$

$10 = 4 + 4 + 4^0 + 4^0$

$11 = 4 + 4 + 4 - 4^0$

$12 = 4^2 - 4 - 4 + 4$

$13 = 4^2 - 4^0 - 4^0 - 4^0$

$14 = 4^2 - 4 + 4^0 + 4^0$

$15 = 4^2 - 4^0 + 4^0 - 4^0$

$16 = 4 + 4 + 4 + 4$

$17 = 4^2 + 4^0 - 4^0 + 4^0$

$18 = (4 \times 4) + 4^0 + 4^0$

$19 = 4^2 + 4^0 + 4^0 + 4^0$

$20 = 4! - 4 + 4 - 4$

CONTENT: Mathematical operations

PROCESSES: Devising methods, improvising, experimenting and checking

N15

# Poetic Pi!

USE the number sequence of Pi to write words in patterns, sentences, or poems.

**3.1415926535**

COMMENT: The first word in the sentence must have 3 letters, the next word 1 letter, the next 4 letters and so on. Have children discuss why their choices are limited.

**1**

YEAR 6
Can I have a large chocolate in France, Italy and Spain?

**2**

YEAR 5
Word pattern: Words begin with 'I'
Ink, I, Inch, I, Image, Important, In, Invent, Irish, Ice, index

**E**

YEAR 6
The 'B' note I sound strumming my guitar makes you happy.

| CONTENT: Pi, 2D shapes, circles, circumference | PROCESSES: Devising methods, inventing, making meaning |
|---|---|

# Word Starters

# W1 Word Pyramid

COMMENT: A lovely opportunity to play with words. Given the initial structure, the children will build their own pyramids, starting with the letter at the top. The letters can either stay in sequence or they could be rearranged when forming the next word.

**1**

YEAR 5

A
A N D
S A N D
H A N D S
D A N I S H
S H I N P A D
P I N H E A D S
H E A D S P I N S

**2**

YEAR 5

A
A N
N A P
P L A N
P L A N T
P L A N E T
P L A N E T S

CONTENT: Spelling, vocabulary

PROCESSES: Assessing alternatives, devising methods, recognising patterns

W2

# Word Associations

| | |
|---|---|
| **RED** | **APPLE** |
| **APPLE** | **FRUIT** |
| **FRUIT** | **HEALTHY** |

COMMENT: Start with any two words. The list that develops is endless. To make it more challenging, the list could be limited to things in school, or in a park, or things that are round, and so on. This starter can also be played verbally, round the classroom – very enjoyable for little ones!

## 1

YEAR 1

White Black
Black Zebra
Zebra Horse
Horse Dog
Dog Cat
Cat Mouse
Mouse Rat
Rat Fat

## 2

YEAR 5

Top Hat
Hat Head
Head Brain
Brain 5S
5S Thinking
Thinking School
School Fun
Fun Happy
Happy Talk

Talk Mouth
Mouth Neck
Neck Shoulders
Shoulders Arms
Arms Body
Body Legs
Legs Feet
Feet Socks
Socks Shoes

And so on to over 100 associations

CONTENT: Immediate thoughts, associations

PROCESSES: Connecting, recognising patterns

# W3 Four Letter Words

CHANGE one letter at a time, to make as many different four-letter words as possible.

**BOOK**

COMMENT: The starting word could be anything at all, although some have more scope than others. Children could experiment with their own starting word, maybe even trying to loop back to the beginning. Children should recognise the letter patterns they rely on the most.

**1**

YEAR 4

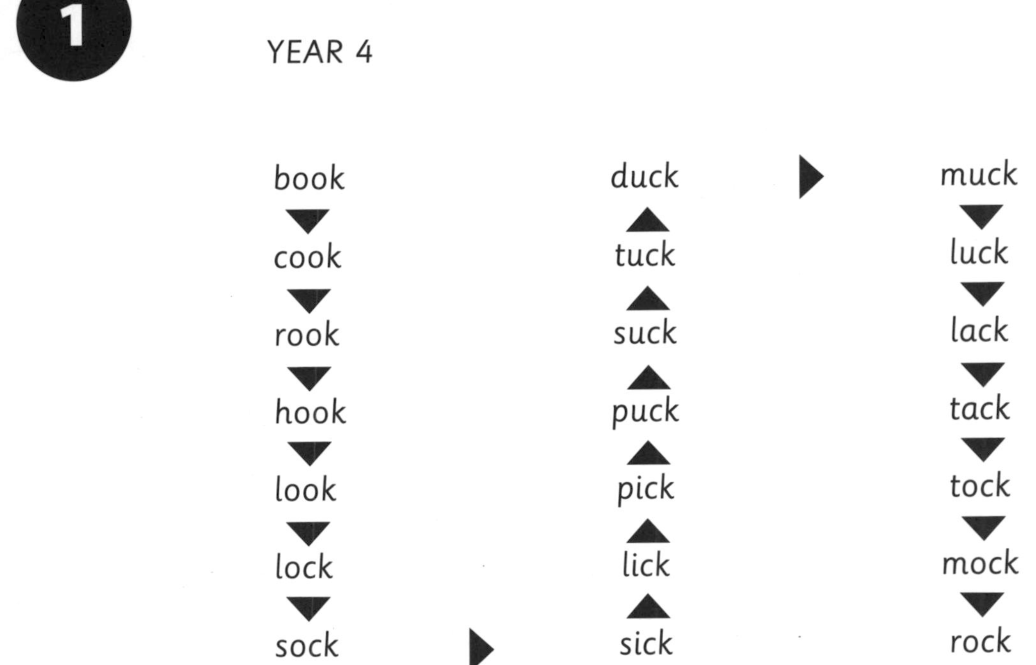

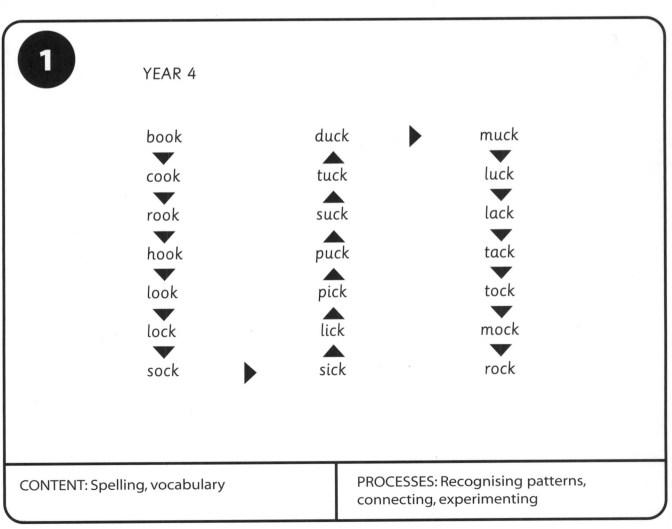

CONTENT: Spelling, vocabulary

PROCESSES: Recognising patterns, connecting, experimenting

W4

# Number Story

WRITE a story using the numbers 1–10.

**One day, there were two children who lived at 3 Park Street....**

COMMENT: An enjoyable challenge with enormous potential for follow ups and the reinforcement of various aspects of story writing in subsequent literacy lessons.

**1**

YEAR 3

*Once upon a time there was one girl who lived at number 2 White Ladies Road. This girl has 3 friends called Phoebe, Jacob and Harriet. She had 4 aunts and 5 uncles. Also she had 6 cousins and 7 hamsters. Some of them were babies. She had to go 8 miles to get to school. It took 9 minutes on the bus. If she walked it took 10 minutes.*

**2**

YEAR 5

*Once I saw 10 people shopping. 2 people went into AllSports while 5 went into John Lewis. I was buying a vanilla ice-cream and 3 others were having a McDonalds. 9 people were chatting and 8 were watching the fountain. 4 people were coming out of the Bear Factory with 7 following. 6 were leaving with everyone following them.*

| CONTENT: Story writing and planning | PROCESSES: Devising methods, experimenting and checking, improvising |
|---|---|

W5

# Double Meaning

WHAT WORD makes sense with both?

**bus [stop] shouting**
**car [park] benches**

COMMENT: A lovely one for children of all ages. After a few examples, the children could easily make up their own.

**1**

YEAR 4

dinner [party] food

school [time] flies

keep [working] model

my [mind] games

**2**

YEAR 5

library [book] worm

nettle [rash] decision

heavy [fine] works

CONTENT: Connections, associations

PROCESSES: Experiment and check, recognising patterns, connecting

## W6 Easter Time

THINK of egg words!

**Eggcellent!**
**Eggciting!**
**Eggspect**

COMMENT: Pure fun, and very useful whenever there is an egg-related event!

**1**

YEAR 5

Eggstra
Eggsit
Eggseptional
Eggsercise
Eggstravaganza
Eggsecuted
Eggstremely
Eggsactly
Eggstreme
Eggspensive
Eggsibit
Eggsperience
Eggsperiment
Eggsplained
Eggcetera
Eggcitement
Eggs-ray
Eggspectations
Eggschange
The eggs-factor

CONTENT: Easter, celebrations

PROCESSES: Inventing

# W7 Letter Jumble

USE these letters to make as many new words as possible.

**WORLD POETRY DAY**

COMMENT: This one is very useful to mark special occasions and celebrations. Depending on the age of the children, the letters that they are choosing from could be used more than once or just the number of times they actually appear. The theme could also be restricted to a particular topic area, such as scientific words as above.

**1**

YEAR 4

Starter: Westbury Park Primary School

| | |
|---|---|
| West | Cat |
| Park | South |
| Car | Stamp |
| Sam | Colour |
| Many | People |
| Rap | Picture |
| Rat | Scramble |
| The | Ate |

**2**

YEAR 5

Starter: World Poetry Day

| | |
|---|---|
| We | Red |
| Try | Row |
| Dad | Tow |
| Pet | Road |
| Poet | Pool |
| Rod | Pot |
| Tray | Read |
| Door | Pea |

**3**

YEAR 6

Starter: Westbury Park Primary School

| | |
|---|---|
| Spooky | Rules |
| Best Curry | Bury pets School |
| Beauty school | Rusty School |
| Cool | Work lots |
| Spike | Rosemary |
| Ark | |

CONTENT: Science week, celebrations, spelling

PROCESSES: Experimenting and checking, devising methods, assessing alternatives

W8

# Acrostic

USE the name of a special occasion, topic or celebration to write an acrostic poem.

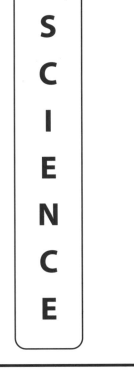

S
C
I
E
N
C
E

**1**

YEAR 4

Solids

Cells

Insulators

Engineering

Nurse

Chemistry

Electricity

**2**

YEAR 5

Solids and liquids,

Chemistry too!

Investigations just for you.

Enter the week when we celebrate

National science week.

Can you think of something science is about?

Enter the world of science and

you will find out.

CONTENT: Poetry, acrostics

PROCESSES: Experimenting and checking, assessing alternatives, making meaning

W9

# Double Acrostic

T I G E R S

USE a special occasion, topic or celebration to write an acrostic poem where each line starts and ends with the same letter. Make up your own starting word.

T I G E R S

1

YEAR 6

*Tigers are greaT*
*I like them because I*
*Get excited because their jaws are like a peG*
*Every timE*
*Running fast theiR*
*Stripes help them catch creatureS*

COMMENT: Poetry, acrostics

PROCESSES: Experimenting and checking, assessing alternatives, improvising

## W10 Imaginative Initials

WHAT DO your initials stand for?

**E.O.S: excellent olympic swimmer**
**T.P.S: tennis player supreme**

CONTENT: This one makes children feel very special, particularly if they can create sentences that actually apply to them and highlight their particular skills and interests. They love creating ones for teachers!

**1**

YEAR 1 (after whole-class discussion)

1. Beatrice Bacon (B.B) Beautiful Butterfly
2. Gabriel Vickerman (G.V) Great Vampire
3. Robbie McCleod (R.M.) Robot Marvellous
4. Lukha Aggarwaal (L.A.) London Alligator
5. Ella Parsons (E.P.) Extremely Pretty
6. Thomas Staricoff (T.S) Tennis Star

COMMENT: Initials, acronyms

PROCESSES: Inventing, assessing alternatives, making meaning, improvising

# W11 Word Chain

CREATE a sentence in which each word begins with the last letter of the previous word.

**At this school, learning gives such happiness!**

COMMENT: This is very challenging but can be extremely rewarding for children once they get into the swing of it. It works very well as a small-group task.

**1**

YEAR 5

*My yellow watch has seven numbers.*

*Dig giant turnips superbly.*

*Some eagles swim amazingly.*

CONTENT: Sentence structure, spelling

PROCESSES: Assessing alternatives, experimenting and checking

W12

# Even Writing

THE ALPHABET could be divided into 'even' and 'odd' letters: A is even, B is odd, C is even, D is odd and so on. Create words or sentences made up only of 'even' letters.

**Ace (Even)**

COMMENT: It is so interesting to play with words! Very soon the children discover that all vowels just happen to be even. Start by making a key. Can there be any 'odd' words?

**1**

YEAR 4

I am sick (Even)

I am a yoyo (Even)

Amy is sick (Even)

Will is sick (Even)

**2**

YEAR 5

Ace (Even)

Is (Even)

Ways (Even)

Eyes (Even)

I was (Even)

As I was seven, I was sick (Even)

CONTENT: Sentence structure, spelling, odd/even

PROCESSES: Experimenting and checking, devising methods

# W13 Acronyms

CREATE your own Acronyms. What do they stand for?

**NTIC: No Talking in Class!**
**NSR: Non Smoking Restaurant**

COMMENT: These could be anything at all. They could be related to topics created by visits. The children really like guessing each others' although they may need a few clues. Discuss with children what makes a good acronym.

**1**

YEAR 5

1. RAC Rabbit Association Cars
2. AA Atrocious Accidents
3. QEH Questions Eat Ham
4. BGS Big Grape School
5. PDSA Panthers Dip Soppy Apples
6. SAS Sing and Sign

| CONTENT: Acronyms | PROCESSES: Inventing, making associations, devising methods, giving reasons |
|---|---|

W14

# Starts and Ends

THINK of words that start and end with the same letter.

**Argentina**

COMMENT: There are lots of countries and continents that do this, so it may be a good one to link to the humanities.

**1**

YEAR 5

| | | |
|---|---|---|
| Alexandra | That | Recorder |
| Sports | Thought | Tent |
| Eye | Africa | America |
| Envelope | Pop | Sandwiches |
| Skills | Hannah | Extreme |
| Europe | Ruler | Remember |
| Diamond | Nun | Ease |
| Amnesia | Australia | Did |
| Area | Classic | Stains |

CONTENT: Spelling, vocabulary

PROCESSES: Ordering, devising methods, assessing alternatives

# A-Z

## Create an A-Z of...

COMMENT: There is no better, more versatile and more useful starter than this one. It can be applied to absolutely anything one is doing, and the children can't get enough of it! An A to Z can be used for any topic as the example shows.

**1**

YEAR 1: SCHOOL

A: Asssembly
B: Books,
C: Concentrating, capacity
D: Drawing
E: End of the year, experiment
F: Fun, football
G: Garden shop (home corner)
H: Home corner
I: ICT
J: Jumping
K: Kicking a football
L: Literacy
M: Music
N: Numeracy
O: One hundred blocks
P: Philosophy, planning, PE, playtime
Q: Quiet
R: Reading
S: Sweets, symmetry, sports day, science
T: Terrific work, TV
U: Umbrella mending (materials topic)
V: Victorians
W: Work
X: Xavier second in running race
Y: Yummy food at the class party
Z: Zach winning all his races

| CONTENT: A-Z, brainshowers, summaries, alphabet | PROCESSES: Devising methods, improvising, ordering, imagining |
| --- | --- |

# W16 Titles and Authors

THINK of book titles with related author names.

**Stolen Money by Robin Banks**

COMMENT: This is one of the children's favourites. They can make up any book titles and we have found that it is sometimes very difficult to stop laughing when we share their ideas.

YEAR 4

Gardening by I. Dig

The biology of spiders by R.U. Web

A cold winter's night by I.C Frost

The Christmas present by U. Wrap

2

YEAR 5

Wildlife by Amir Kat

Gardening by A. Plant

A cold winter's night by I. Shiver

A green garden by Eva Green

Hot drinks by A. Capuchino

CONTENT: Books, titles, authors

PROCESSES: Devising methods, inventing, imagining

# W17 The Whole Alphabet

## Write a sentence or sentences using all the letters of the alphabet

COMMENT: A wonderful challenge that uses their imagination. It promotes a systematic approach to problem solving and is very rewarding when achieved, especially if the sentences make sense!

**1**

YEAR 5

*I went to see my grandma who lives in Bristol. I live in London along with the Queen. Sadly I couldn't bring my pet fox on holiday because my grandma doesn't approve of him. She thinks he should be in a zoo, so my friends Katharine and James are looking after him.*

| CONTENT: Sentence structure, spelling, alphabet | PROCESSES: Devising methods, experimenting and checking, improvising |
|---|---|

# W18 Alphabetical Sentences

WRITE one or more sentences where the first word begins with a, the second with b, the third with c, and so on. How far along the alphabet can you get?

**A brown car drove eight friends ...**

COMMENT: It is important for the children to try and make sense with these, otherwise they will just write words at random.

**1**

YEAR 5

*A bug called Derek eats fried grass.*

*A boy called Dan electrocuted four girls. He is jailed.*

| CONTENT: Sentence structure, spelling, alphabet | PROCESSES: Devising methods, experimenting and checking, improvising |
|---|---|

W19

# Alphabetical Words

THINK of words where all the letters in the word are in alphabetical order!

**Act, mops, best ...**

COMMENT: The letters don't need to be in consecutive order. It is interesting to see who can think of the longest word!

**1**

YEAR 4

| | |
|---|---|
| Hills | Know |
| Alps | Bins |
| Bills | Fins |
| Abby | Been |
| Forty | Knot |
| Boot | Beers |
| Foot | Deer |
| Cells | Chops |
| Gills | Dos (Spanish) |
| Adders | Adios (Spanish) |

| | |
|---|---|
| CONTENT: Sentence structure, spelling, alphabet | PROCESSES: Devising methods, experimenting and checking, improvising |

# Science Starters

S1 **The Meaning of Science** 

## What does science mean to you?

COMMENT: It is interesting to allow children the opportunity to think about science in the real world and about the contributions it makes to our everyday lives. It is actually very hard to think of something that does not, in some way or other, involve science or scientists. Enjoy!

YEAR 4

WHAT IS SCIENCE?

*Science is trying to find out about the world and answer questions through experiments. A question could be: 'How fast can water cool down?' Then you would record the results.*

*Science can also be about the human body and how things work. It can also be about space and what happens in the world and why it happens. You can also have a job that can be to do with science: a scientist, doctor, nurse or vet. The doctor uses science because it is about the human body and trying to make it work again.*

| CONTENT: The nature of science | PROCESSES: Making meaning, valuing, connecting |
|---|---|

# S2 Does size matter?

## Create a list of things that get progressively larger or smaller

COMMENT: This one can be enjoyed by children of any age. They will try and compete to see who can manage the longest sequence. To make it more challenging, the list could be restricted to a particular topic.

**1**

YEAR 2

| | |
|---|---|
| Flea | Sheep |
| Ant | Wallaby |
| Mouse | Camel |
| Fish | Elephant |
| Rabbit | Dolphin |
| Cat | Great White Shark |
| Dog | Blue Whale |

**2**

YEAR 5

| | |
|---|---|
| Ant | Human |
| Millipede | Dolphin |
| Cockroach | Shark |
| Cod | Bull |
| Jellyfish | Giraffe |
| Golden Eagle | Elephant |
| Cheetah | Whale |

CONTENT: Size, measure, metric system

PROCESSES: Comparing, visualising

S3

# Is Science in Everything?

## Can you think of anything that does not involve science?

COMMENT: A wonderful way of highlighting the importance of science and scientists to our society. This will really test the children. Most things will have some connection to science!

**1**

YEAR 6

*It is probably impossible to find something not to do with science like it is with maths. What about nothingness?*

*Some things don't seem to have anything to do with science but they do if you think about them.*

WRITING *The process of making the paper.*

*The ink is a chemical and it is made.*

*Computers depend on scientific inventions from the past.*

*How do our brains think about what to write?*

*How do our hands know where to move?*

| CONTENT: The nature of science | PROCESSES: Imagining, connecting |
|---|---|

# S4 Science and the Modern World

## How does science contribute to our society?

COMMENT: This also highlights value of science in society. The list can include direct links, chains of links or links to specific professions.

### 1

YEAR 5

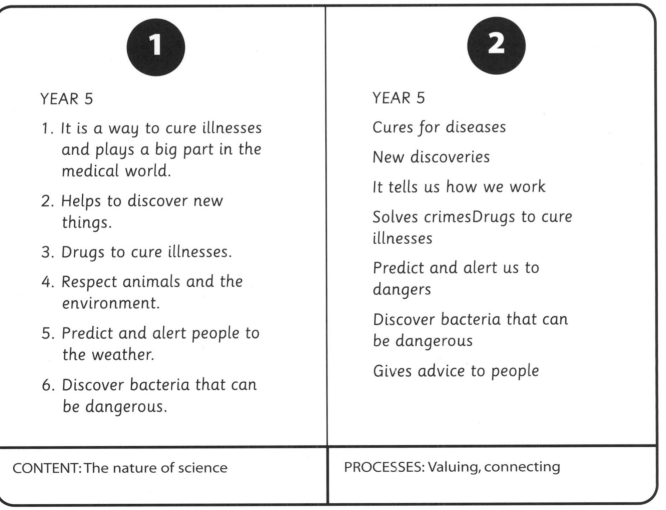

1. It is a way to cure illnesses and plays a big part in the medical world.
2. Helps to discover new things.
3. Drugs to cure illnesses.
4. Respect animals and the environment.
5. Predict and alert people to the weather.
6. Discover bacteria that can be dangerous.

### 2

YEAR 5

Cures for diseases

New discoveries

It tells us how we work

Solves crimesDrugs to cure illnesses

Predict and alert us to dangers

Discover bacteria that can be dangerous

Gives advice to people

CONTENT: The nature of science

PROCESSES: Valuing, connecting

# S5 Science Mind Map

## Create a Mind Map of …

This one assumes the children are familiar with the concept of Mind Mapping, devised by Tony Buzan. The map itself could be about anything at all: the current topic, a future topic, opinions or ethical issues.

**1**

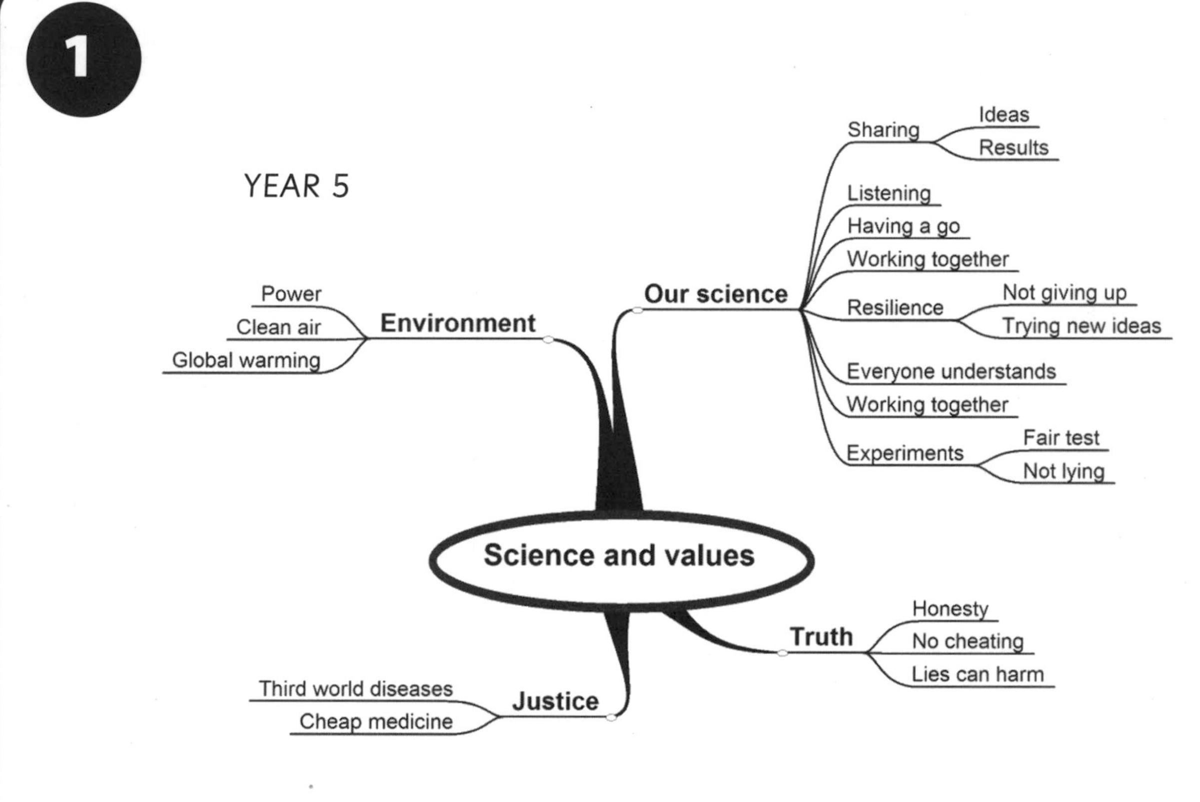


| CONTENT: Mind Maps, the issue in question | PROCESSES: Remembering, visualising, classifying |
|---|---|

S6

# A Doctor's Life

## Create a list of all the different illnesses and diseases you can think of

COMMENT: A fascinating insight into how lucky we are when everything is okay. This challenge helps to prepare for discussion on health-related topics and for any visits from doctors or scientists to the school. It is interesting to ask children to categorise the illnesses and diseases accoring to their own categories

**1**

YEAR 1 (after discussion in class)

Cancer

Tummy ache

Headache

Cough

Cold

Toothache

Tonsillitis

Earache

Chicken pox

Death!

**2**

YEAR 5

CATEGORIES

Things that kill you
Things that don't kill you

Symptoms you can see
Symptoms you can't see

Diseases caused by germs
Diseases not caused by germs

CONTENT: Healthy living, ourselves, disease

PROCESSES: Remembering, classifying, comparing

# S7 A Risky Life

## What risks do we all take during our everyday lives?

COMMENT: The way children perceive risk is fascinating! Everything carries a certain degree of risk. Some of our worries about risks are rational, but some activities are perceived as very risky when they are actually relatively safe. Children could go on to place their activities on a line representing degrees of risk.

Maximum risk |————————————| No risk

**1**

YEAR 4

FROM NOT RISKY TO VERY RISKY

1. Pick up a book
2. Stand still
3. Bicycle
4. Run on a dry floor
5. Swimming
6. Run on a wet floor
7. Boxing
8. Parachuting
9. Climbing mountains
10. Swimming with sharks

| CONTENT: Risk, health and safety | CONTENT: Ordering, comparing, imagining, giving reasons |
|---|---|

# S8 States of Matter

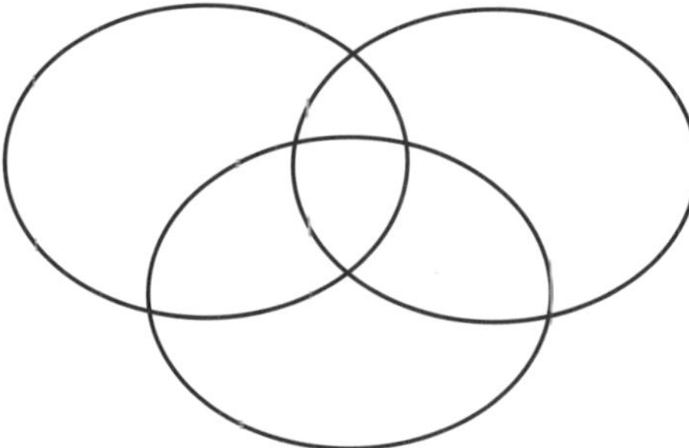

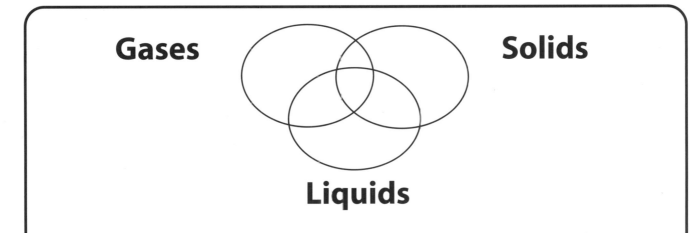


COMMENT: All children can have a go at this challenge but the outcome will be very dependent on age. This challenge is a particularly useful compliment to the study of states of matter. Amazing things can happen with this one, such as children wondering where fire and electricity should go! An understanding of Venn diagrams is required.

**1**

YEAR 5

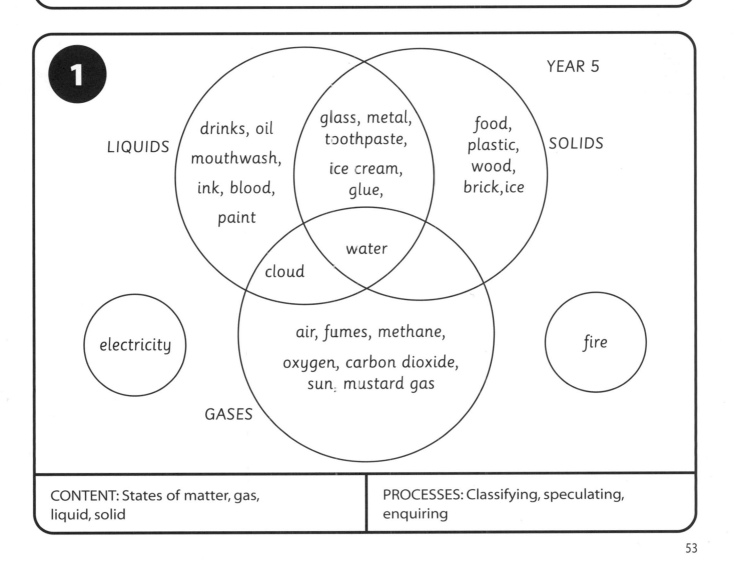

LIQUIDS: drinks, oil mouthwash, ink, blood, paint

LIQUIDS and SOLIDS: glass, metal, toothpaste, ice cream, glue,

SOLIDS: food, plastic, wood, brick, ice

LIQUIDS and GASES: cloud

LIQUIDS, SOLIDS and GASES: water

GASES: air, fumes, methane, oxygen, carbon dioxide, sun, mustard gas

electricity

fire

| CONTENT: States of matter, gas, liquid, solid | PROCESSES: Classifying, speculating, enquiring |
| --- | --- |

# S9 Science Scrabble

## Play Science Scrabble!

COMMENT: Children can play by themselves or with a friend, using squared paper, and writing one letter per square following Scrabble rules. They are only allowed to use scientific words, or words that they associate with a particular science topic. Children working in pairs using different colours will leave a very impressive board!

**1** YEAR 5



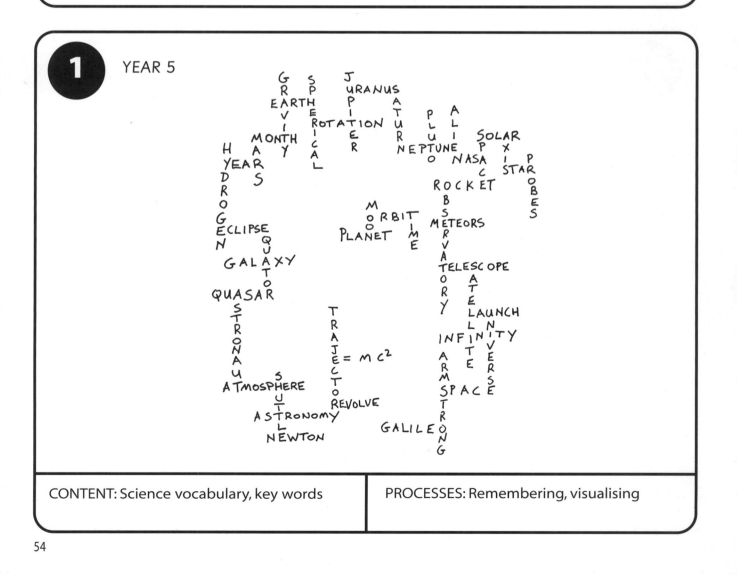

CONTENT: Science vocabulary, key words

PROCESSES: Remembering, visualising

S10

# Famous Discoveries

## What do you think are the most valuable scientific discoveries?

COMMENT: This is a good starter for enquiry at home. It is a wonderful way of highlighting the importance of science and scientists to our society. The list can include present-day discoveries or ones from the past. Some children may wish to rank these in terms of their 'value to society'. Ask them to give reasons for their choices.

**1**

YEAR 5

Abacus (500BC) Crossbow (1050) Lighthouse (280BC) Cooker (1679) Wheelbarrow (230 BC) Pencil (1565)

Magnifying glass (1250) Watch (1504) Telescope (1668) Submarine (1620) Rocket (1100) Printing press (1454)

| CONTENT: The nature of science, discoveries, scientists | PROCESSES: Remembering, enquiring, valuing, giving reasons |
| --- | --- |

# S11 Famous Scientists

## Create a list of famous scientists

COMMENT: This is a good starter or enquiry at home. The list can include present-day scientists or ones from the past. Some children may also know why they have become. You could also ask the children to categorise the scientists according to 'inventors' and 'discoverers'.

1

YEAR 5

Isaac Newton: gravity

Felix Hoffman: aspirin

Thomas Edison: the light bulb

Einstein: Relativity $e=mc^2$

Alexander Graham Bell: telephone

Thomas Crapper: flush toilet

Wright Brothers: aviators

John Logie Baird: physics (TV)

Jane Wright: cancer research

| CONTENT: Scientists, inventions | PROCESSES: Remembering, enquiring, valuing, categorising |
|---|---|

S12

# Our Planets

## Create your own mnemonic to remember the sequence of the planets

COMMENT: Children will really enjoy creating a mnemonic that is personal and will help them or the rest of the class remember the sequence and order of the planets. Discuss with the children what makes a good mnemonic. Which of their mnemonics are easy to remember? Why?

**1**

YEAR 5

Mercury Venus Earth Mars Jupiter Saturn Uranus Neptune Pluto

My very easy maths job sometimes uses nuclear physics

My vase eating monster juggles saucers under naughty ponies.

Many violent earthlings munch jumping sandwiches under naughty pillows.

My violent elbow might just smack unaware naughty Peter.

My violent earthling mum juggles sausages using no pottery.

| CONTENT: Planets | PROCESSES: Inventing, remembering, improvising, devising methods |
|---|---|

# S13 Door Knobs

## What are the advantages and disadvantages of having door knobs made out of chocolate?

COMMENT: Children's thinking is very focused in this one. Dealing with a real object and it's uses requires that they think of practical issues. There are links to science, materials, temperature, health and safety and other issues.

YEAR 4

ADVANTAGES

1. It would be yummy.
2. If you run out o your own food you can eat the doorknobs.
3. They would be easier to replace.
4. It would be easier to make another one.

DISADVANTAGES

1. When you have hot hands and open the door, your hands will get sticky.
2. Eventually it would crumble to pieces.
3. If you eat it you will be locked in.
4. It wouldn't last as long as a wooden one.
5. It gets germs on easily so you could get ill if you eat it.
6. It might snap off when you open it.

| CONTENT: Materials, chocolate, states of matter | PROCESSES: Imagining consequences, assessing alternatives, speculating |
|---|---|

# S14 Energy Saver

## In what ways are we able to save energy?

COMMENT: The issue of energy consumption and conservation is a fascinating one. How do we use or misuse our energy supplies? This can lead to a wonderful discussion on alternative sources of obtaining our energy. Each 'solution' gives further scope for questioning and enquiry.

**1**

YEAR 4

WAYS OF SAVING ENERGY

1. Have solar powered aeroplanes.
2. Solar-powered lights.
4. Put pans on top of each other on the cooker.
5. Keep lights off during the day.
6. Use bikes to travel around.
7. Have showers not baths because baths use too much hot water.
8. Use a piano not a keyboard.
9. Open curtains instead of using lights
10. Wear more clothes instead of turning on the heating.
12. Turn off electricity appliances when you are not using them.

| CONTENT: Energy, renewable resources | PROCESSES: Speculating, giving reasons, imagining consequences |
|---|---|

# S15 Outer Space

## Things found in outer space

CONTENT: This list will include both the obvious and obscure. It has the potential to really surprise you. Some children's knowledge of space is quite outstanding!

**1**

YEAR 3

Shooting stars

Comets

Planets

Milky Way

Constellations

Moon

Rockets

The sun

The universe

**2**

YEAR 5

Dark side of the moon

Astronauts

American flag on the moon

Satellites

A lack of atmosphere

Footprints

Methane gas

Debris from the space shuttle

Black holes

Stars

Meteorites

CONTENT: Space, planets

PROCESSES: Speculating, remembering, imagining, enquiring

# S16 Blood and Ketchup

## What are the similarities and differences between blood and ketchup?

COMMENT: This is one of the best starters because, although it seems slightly crazy at first, the act of comparing these two items often leads children into posing a series of interesting questions. Pupils may say that both blood and ketchup are man-made but what do they mean by 'man-made' in each case? Is blood 'made' and, if so, what is it made from? Discussion sessions following this starter give plenty of opportunities for you to ask questions to get children fascinated by the topic.

**1**

YEAR 5

| SIMILARITIES | DIFFERENCES |
|---|---|
| Both are red | Blood is thinner |
| Both have sugar in them | Blood is darker |
| Both are used by people | Blood is made in the body and ketchup in a factory |
| Both are man-made (but in different ways) | You can't eat blood |
| They can both be inside your body | Ketchup is made out of tomatoes, blood isn't. |
| | You need blood to live, but not ketchup. |
| | You don't bleed ketchup. |

| CONTENTS: The human body, ourselves, healthy living | PROCESSES: Comparing, enquiring, connecting, questioning |
|---|---|

# S17 Future Directions

**What do you think should be the next**
**• invention**
**• discovery**
**• cure**
**for scientists to strive for?**

COMMENT: It is interesting to see where children's priorities lie. They will rely on personal experiences opening up interesting avenues for follow-up discussions.

**1**

YEAR 5

To discover if there's life on Mars.

To discover viable electricity supplies.

A cure for cancer.

A cure for AIDS.

Discover other solar systems.

Cars that run on water.

Effective and affordable warning systems for natural disasters.

| CONTENT: Inventions, discoveries | PROCESSES: Improvising, valuing, prioritising, giving reasons |
|---|---|

# Philosophy Starters

# Laughter is the Best Medicine

## Things that make you laugh!

COMMENT: There is nothing more rewarding than starting the day discussing what makes children happy. Some of the answers could be very deep, some very personal, and some very obscure at first, until explained! A great one to encourage humour in the classroom. Why do certain kinds of things make us happy? Are there similarities in people lists?

YEAR 1

People tickling me

People telling me jokes

My little sister

My Dad

Finding funny things when we're spying in the playground

Standing on one finger in the baby pool

Xavier's made up song

Talking in a made-up language

2

YEAR 4

Some jokes

Being chased

Being tickled

Joe's hiccups

My sister Kate

Mary Poppins

Terrible TV programmes

My family

My brother's emails

Mum's puddle fish impression

3

YEAR 5

A-H of what makes me laugh

Accents

Beano

Crabs

Donkeys

Eggs

Frogs

Good Jokes

Humour

CONTENT: Laughter, happiness, wellbeing

PROCESSES: Remembering, generalising, questioning, giving reasons

P2

# Wish, Wish, Wish

## If you could grant the world five wishes, what would they be?

COMMENT: It is interesting to compare wishes children would like for themselves, for the school, for their town and for the world. Are they the same or different?

**1**

YEAR 5

WORLD WISHES

Peace

Safe food and water

End to poverty

Everyone to be healthy

Everyone to have a good education

**2**

YEAR 4

PERSONAL WISHES

I would wish for a tamagotchie

I would wish for a puppy or kitten

I would wish for a younger sister

I would wish for loads of money

I would wish for my own room

CONTENT: The world, environment

PROCESSES: Remembering, generalising, questioning, giving reasons

P3

# Spoon Fed

## Questions you would ask a spoon

COMMENT: This is an absolute classic and has stimulated some of the most original and humorous pieces of thinking from children. Giving them one or two examples will set them off wonderfully. After doing this one you would be able to think of similar variants. It's a great way of exploring different kinds of questions with children.

YEAR 3

Do you like being sucked?

Did a cow jump over you?

What is your favourite food?

Are you famous?

Are sweet things your favourite foods?

Do you love the knife or the fork?

Do you get catapulted?

Who is your best friend?

2

YEAR 4

Do you get dizzy when we stir you?

Do you speak a different language?

What is your name?

Did it hurt when you were cut into shape?

What tree did you come from?

Does it hurt when people dip you in hot soup?

CONTENT: Questioning

PROCESSES: Questioning, imagining, improvising, inventing

P4

# Questions, Questions

## What questions can you think of that do not have an answer, or that have more than one answer?

COMMENT: This one is for children who love to ask big questions about life. Moral dilemmas with more than one possible solution are facinating. These are great starting points for more developed philosophical discussions with a class.

**1**

YEAR 5

How did the world begin?

Is there extraterrestrial life?

How many undiscovered species are there?

Why do we dream?

How did life begin?

Does nothing exist?

Does God exist?

What is the shape of the universe?

What is the point of life?

Should we have zoos?

**2**

YEAR 6

Where does space end?

Why is our language so complicated?

Why do so many places have different languages and accents?

Why are we the only really sophisticated animals?

CONTENT: Philosophy

PROCESSES: Questioning, speculating, enquiring

P5

# A Perfect World

## A recipe for a perfect world

COMMENT: The children will love do do this one as an actual recipe! It is amazing how wonderful their desires are. You could extend the activity by asking how they would 'cook' the dish. So, if one ingredient is 'love', how could people bring love into the world?

1

YEAR 4

A recipe for a perfect world

300g of love

600g of peace

A handful of sunshine

100g of friendship

200g of sunshine

100% no war

100% no murder

| CONTENT: Our world, environment, metaphors | PROCESSES: Prioritising, imaging, visualising |
|---|---|

# P6 Peaceful Times

## Why do wars happen?

COMMENT: Children have an amazing ability to think about the world in a sensible matter of fact way. This starter brings out some some simple but perceptive suggestions. It is a great one to develop further discussions about the alternatives to war and why wars still happen despite the alternatives. Analogies could be made to playground fights between children. Why do they happen when the alternative forms of resolving conflicts are much more desirable?

**1**

YEAR 5

We go to war because countries disagree.

We go to war because one country wants to take over a piece of land.

We go to war because of terrorist attacks like September 11th.

A strike might start a civil war.

A war might start because of religion

Because people aren't happy with what they've got.

| CONTENT: Our world, wars, conflict | PROCESSES: Imagining, valuing |
|---|---|

P7

# Red Nose Day

## What would you spend the money on?

COMMENT: This can be done with any fund raising event. The question really highlights the plight of the world and asks what our priorities should be. It helps us appreciate what we've got and how lucky we are. Ask the children to give reasons for their choices and rank them.

**1**

YEAR 5

CHOICES

Charity in Africa

Charity in the UK

Salvation Army

Food for animals

Hospitals in Africa

Water pumps

Things to make us safer

Endangered species

CHOICES RANKED AND GROUPED

CHARITY IN AFRICA
Hospitals in Africa
Water pumps

CHARITY IN THE UK
Salvation Army

THINGS TO MAKE US SAFER

ANIMALS
Food for animals
Endangered species

CONTENT: Charity, fund raising events

PROCESSES: Imagining consequences, giving reasons, classifying

P8

# Lottery Time

## If you won the Jackpot, how would you spend the money ?

COMMENT: This one is very similar to Red Nose Day (P7), but brings in a personal perspective. What are their priorities and values when it comes to their own money. Ask the pupils to give reasons and rank their ideas.

1

YEAR 5

20% Tsunami Appeal

3% Buy my Family a Country House

10% Children in Need

3% Gift to each of my family

10% More Lottery Tickets

10% Aston Martin Cars

20% Countries without fresh water

20% Mum to retire

4% Friends

| CONTENT: Money, finance | PROCESSES: Imagining consequences, giving reasons, prioritising |
|---|---|

P9

# Election Time

## What would your priorities be if you were to stand for...?

COMMENT: A superb way to prepare for school council speeches and to discuss real values in our society. Sharing these can be very illuminating.

**1**

YEAR 4

STANDING FOR SCHOOL COUNCIL

Healthier more enjoyable school dinners

More opportunity to develop sport in primary schools

Adventurous, safe playground with more grass, lots of equipment and organised games

Nicer toilets

More contact with local secondary schools

**2**

YEAR 4

STANDING FOR MP

Initiatives to reduce pollution

Working towards a more peaceful world

Protecting endangered species

Better and more hospitals

More recycling opportunities

Safer roads

Housing and food for all

More help to poorer countries

CONTENT: Elections, manifestos

PROCESSES: Valuing, prioritising, giving reasons

# P10 On a Different Planet

**If you were responsible for setting up life on a new planet, what values would you like the people moving there to have?**

COMMENT: This will lead to whole-class discussions about school values, family values and, with older ones, the rights and wrongs of the society we live in. Make sure children give reasons for their choices and think up some examples of their values in action.

YEAR 6

| ✓ | ✗ |
|---|---|
| Peace<br>Honesty<br>Friendship<br>Hope<br>Love<br>Trust<br>Self confidence<br>Respect<br>Tolerance | Weapons<br>Smoking<br>Excessive drinking<br>Killing<br>Swearing<br>Wars<br>Illegal drugs<br>Illness |

CONTENT: Our world, environment, society

PROCESSES: Prioritising, valuing, generalising, giving reasons

# P11 All alone

## If you were alone for a week, which 3 songs, 3 objects and 3 books would you like to have with you? Why?

COMMENT: This challenge helps to highlight what is really important to the children in their lives. Asking them to justify their responses also helps them to talk about their personal lives and interests. The things to be chosen can be changed to whatever you wish.

**1**

YEAR 5



**2**

YEAR 5



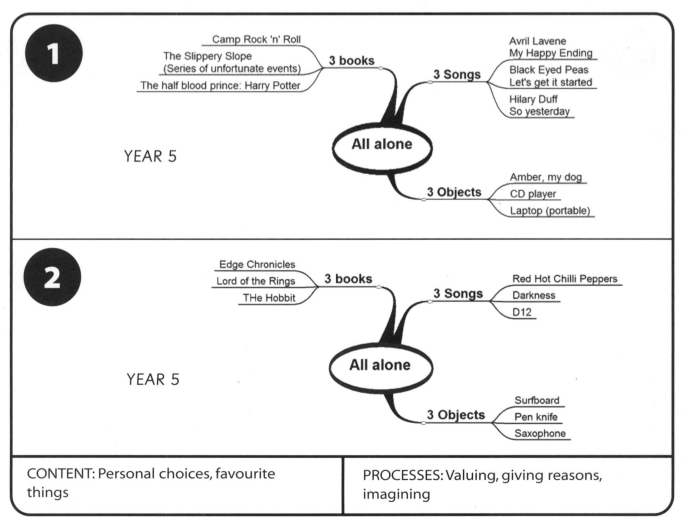

| CONTENT: Personal choices, favourite things | PROCESSES: Valuing, giving reasons, imagining |
| --- | --- |

P12

# Dinner Party

## You are hosting a dinner party. Who would you invite and why?

COMMENT: A similar task to 'All Alone'. This one allows children to think creatively of people they admire or want to be with. They might even want to invite someone they don't admire but would like to interrogate. The reasons for inviting the guests could be endless – and they could be dead or alive. The characters chosen could be used for a hot-seating exercise. The whole dinner could be acted out. It is another activity that gives an insight into what children value. You could have them categorise the kinds of people they wish to invite and talk about why they value those kinds of people and not others.

YEAR 1 (after class discussion with the teacher)

Spike Milligan (funny)

Einstein (clever)

T-Rex (to eat my house)

Aled and Lydia (to show me how to dance)

The Incredibles (I like them)

Spiderman (to teach me how to climb walls)

David Beckham (my sister likes football)

2

YEAR 5

Piano teacher (entertain)

Friends (play)

Margo Fontaine (ballet heroine)

People at home (not to upset them)

Queen Elizabeth (Control people)

Elvis Presley (sing)

Peter Kay (comedian)

Guy Fawkes (ask him questions)

Henry VIII (ask him about the beheadings)

CONTENT: Friends, famous people

PROCESSES: Valuing, prioritising, giving reasons, evaluating alternatives

# P13 Growing Up is a Hard Thing to Do

## Childhood – Adulthood
## What are the advantages and disadvantages of each?

COMMENT: Fascinating insight into life from the children's perspectives. A great way to find out what they perceive as fair and unfair, what they enjoy, wished they could do, don't ever want to stop doing and so on. It is a great one for comparing results across year groups. All lists will suggest follow-up questions like: 'Why can't adults be cheeky too?' or 'Why is being cheeky an advantage?' Many of the lists reveal a concern with the concept of 'freedom'. It is worth discussing this concept with children. Is freedom always a good thing?

**1** YEAR 3

| ADVANTAGES | |
|---|---|
| CHILD | ADULT |
| You get chocolate | You are in charge |
| You can be cheeky | You can shout |
| You can watch cartoons | You can go to hotels |
| You can buy toys | You have lots of money |
| You get pocket money | You can go out |
| You can play games | You can stay up late |
| You can climb trees | You can go out shopping |
| You can get taken on holiday to Spain | You can wear earrings |

CONTENT: Children, grown-ups

PROCESSES: Comparing, enquiring, valuing, giving reasons

# P14 When I grow up...

## What jobs do you most admire and why?

COMMENT: It is so interesting to find out which jobs children most admire, have respect for, would like to do themselves or regard as beyond their reach. This starter is directly connected to 'Jobs and Society' (P16). These discussions sometimes alert teachers to parents and friends with jobs that could be of interest to children. Inviting adults with different jobs to speak to children can add a lot to the curriculum.

**1**

YEAR 5

Doctors (because they save people's lives).

Scientists (because they find out loads of interesting things as well as medicines).

Comedians and magicians (because they are really good entertainers).

Teachers (because otherwise we wouldn't get a job).

Game designers (because they give us games).

Artists and musicians (because they make us happy).

| CONTENT: Jobs | PROCESSES: Prioritising, giving reasons, imagining, valuing. |
|---|---|

# P15 Heroes and Heroines

## Who are your role models and why?

COMMENT: This one can spring some surprises. Not all children may go for the usual famous characters, but some may choose friends or neighbours. This starter should be fascinating to do and then to follow up with visits from the children's heroes and heroines if possible.

**1**

YEAR 3

| Real Heroes | Made up Heroes |
|---|---|
| Police<br>Firemen<br>Doctors<br>Paramedics<br>Jesus | Batman<br>Spiderman<br>Shrek<br>James Bond<br>Wonder Woman |

My favourite hero is my mum!

She didn't just look after me, she looked after lots of other people.

She never shouts at me even when she is cross.

I was drowning in the deep end of a swimming pool and she saved me.

My mum is my hero because when I am upset she always tries to comfort me.

CONTENT: Famous people, respecting others

PROCESSES: Valuing, giving reasons, assessing alternatives.

# P16 Jobs and Society

## How would you rank the various jobs in terms of importance?

COMMENT: One of my favourites. Is one job more important that another? How does our society value each job? Is the difference in pay between the different jobs fair? After ranking their chosen jobs, the children could try to find out how much people in those jobs are paid. Later, you could provide them with a list of earnings including many of the jobs they chose with some others like 'premiership footballer' for contrast.

**1**

YEAR 3

JOBS IN ORDER OF IMPORTANCE

1. Coastguard
2. Doctor
3. Vet
4. Architect
5. Zoologist
6. Comedian
7. Footballer
8. TV presenter
9. Executioner

**2**

YEAR 5

JOBS IN ORDER OF IMPORTANCE

1. Careworker
2. Doctor
3. Vet
4. Health insurance
5. Shopkeeper
6. Architect
7. Plumber
8. Pilot
9. Zoologist

CONTENT: Jobs

PROCESSES: Prioritising, valuing, giving reasons, speculating

# P17 What are the chances of that?

## Things that will:
## • definitely happen
## • may or may not happen
## • definitely not happen

A fantastic way to introduce or reinforce the concept of probability. This starter also makes children think about the concept of chance and risk, which we tend to take for granted but plays an enormous part in our lives. This starter is directly related to 'A Risky Life' (S7).

YEAR 4

| Definitely happen | May or may not happen | Definitely not happen |
|---|---|---|
| Day will become night<br>Lunch will be at 12.00<br>Break will be at 10.35<br>Someone in the world will die of starvation<br>I will go to bed | I may win the lottery today<br>I may win football<br>Global warming might destroy life on earth<br>It might rain today<br>I might find some money | I won't walk up to school<br>The sun will change colour to blue<br>Sweets will be good for you<br>Apples will be oranges<br>Triangles will be square |

CONTENT: Probability, chance

PROCESSES: Speculating, comparing, imagining

# P18 Lessons in Life

## What lessons has life taught you so far?

COMMENT: The children will bring depth and humour to this one – the perfect blend! The 'lessons' children come up with are good starting points for deeper thinking. If they choose a proverb such as 'look before you leap', have them try to explain it and give examples from life of when it might apply.

**1**

YEAR 5

WHAT LIFE HAS TAUGHT ME

I've learned that:

'I want' doesn't get

If you want friends, be nice to others.

You only live once.

Don't cheat.

A watched kettle doesn't boil.

Look before you leap.

| CONTENT: Our world, life | PROCESSES: Enquiring, generalising, comparing, interpreting |
|---|---|

# P19 For Ever and Ever!

## Things that go on for ever

COMMENT: This starter can get very philosophical (time, space) and also very humorous (parents' nagging). The concept of never ending is fascinating, and is particularly relevant in mathematics; discussing the concept of infinity with a reception class remains a personal teaching highlight!

**1**

YEAR 4
Circle
Life
Recycled can
Earth
Paper
Numbers
School
Food
Water
Inventions

**2**

YEAR 5
Mind Maps
Water Cycle
Numbers
Questions
Universe
Life Cycles
Spirits
Time
Change
Philosophy

CONTENT: Lists, Open-ended

PROCESSES: Speculating, enquiring, imagining

# Creativity Starters

# C1 Anything at all!

## What could each one of these represent?

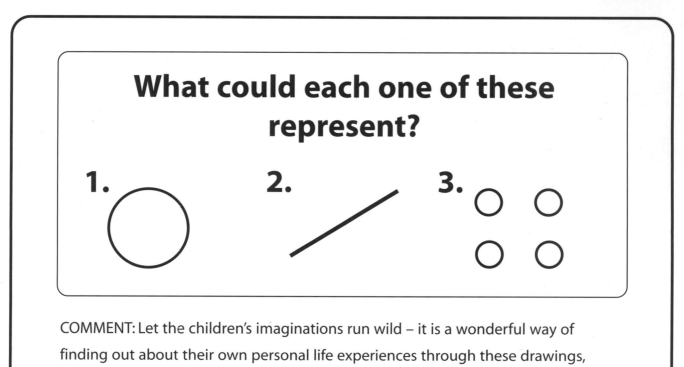

1. 2. 3.

COMMENT: Let the children's imaginations run wild – it is a wonderful way of finding out about their own personal life experiences through these drawings, because what they draw is often connected to their interests or recent activities.

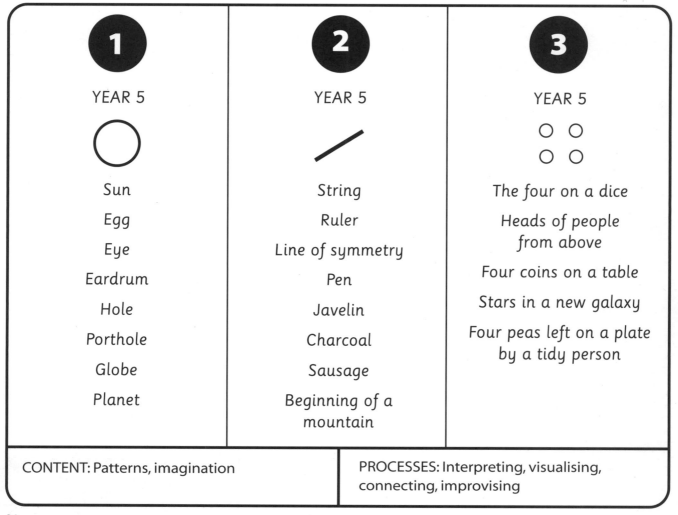

| 1 | 2 | 3 |
|---|---|---|
| YEAR 5 | YEAR 5 | YEAR 5 |
|  |  | |
| Sun<br>Egg<br>Eye<br>Eardrum<br>Hole<br>Porthole<br>Globe<br>Planet | String<br>Ruler<br>Line of symmetry<br>Pen<br>Javelin<br>Charcoal<br>Sausage<br>Beginning of a mountain | The four on a dice<br>Heads of people from above<br>Four coins on a table<br>Stars in a new galaxy<br>Four peas left on a plate by a tidy person |

CONTENT: Patterns, imagination

PROCESSES: Interpreting, visualising, connecting, improvising

C2

# Circle Time

## Starting with a circle what can you end up with?

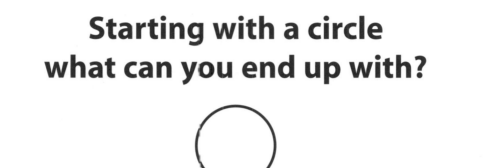

COMMENT: It's amazing how inventive and imaginative children can be. This starter can lead to very interesting discussions. The children's drawings will often represent current classroom topics. You could try the same activity with other combinations of shapes.

CONTENT: Patterns, Imagination

PROCESSES: Visualising, connecting, improvising

# C3 Twinkle Twinkle Little Star

## Make up your own lyrics to Twinkle Twinkle Little Star

COMMENT: Children use the tune of the real song. They just change the words, as in 'twinkle twinkle chocolate bar'. Older ones love to write these for little ones and vice versa!

YEAR 2

*Gurgle, gurgle pot of tar,*
*You will make roads for some cars.*
*Mix it, mix it, pour it out.*
*Make it come from a teapot spout.*

2

YEAR 5

*Yummy, yummy chocolate bar,*
*Please stay here and don't go far.*
*When I buy you from a shop,*
*Ow! my eyes begin to pop.*
*Yummy, yummy chocolate bar,*
*Please stay here and don't go far.*
*When you sit there in a shop,*
*Passers by just have to stop.*
*So yummy yummy chocolate bar*
*Please stay here and don't go far.*

CONTENT: Songs, lyrics, poetry, nursery rhymes

PROCESSES: Assessing alternatives, devising methods, imagining

# C4 Toys Are You

## Invent a new toy

COMMENT: Depending of the age of the children, this starter can be as complex as they would like to make it. It is interesting to vary the activity by suggesting the children invent a toy for different age groups or even adults!

RECEPTION

Alien

An alien that you can turn into anything you choose. It even has a television and lights in its tummy.

YEAR 4

Penguin Sweety Maker

Say 'yummy' and get a nice surprise.

Ask for the flavour you want.

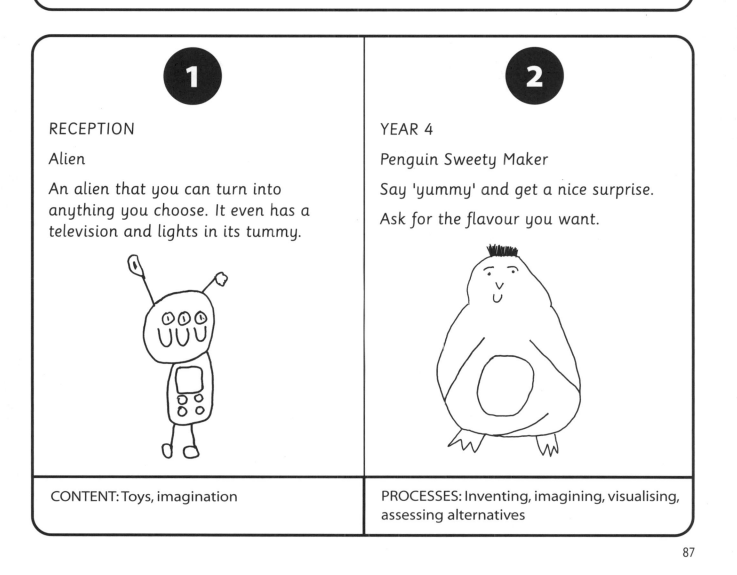

CONTENT: Toys, imagination

PROCESSES: Inventing, imagining, visualising, assessing alternatives

# C5 Inventing Words

## Invent your own words and give their meaning

COMMENT: Children love playing with words and it is very interesting to let them make some up. Their definitions can be very entertaining! Could the children write rules for the others to use when making up new words? They should base the rules on their own inventions.

**1**

YEAR 3

| New word | Definition |
|---|---|
| Ovaralities | Similarities that are obvious |
| Crockle | The sound of an old lady |
| Doft | Soft soil |
| Buggle | To juggle with bugs |

**2**

YEAR 6

| New word | Definition |
|---|---|
| Aquse | Underwater house |
| Femit player | Female cricket player |
| Bodzine | Magazine about the human body |
| Kidologist | Someone who studies kids |

CONTENT: Words, definitions

PROCESSES: Inventing, connecting, assessing alternatives, devising methods

# C6 Guess the Word

## Illustrate an adjective using its first letter only

COMMENT: This starter is a great favourite for those children who are artistically minded and enjoy doodling. It also supports literacy lessons by facilitating the brainstorming of adjectives, or even nouns and verbs. Once they start, the children can not stop!

YEAR 5

COMMENT: Adjectives, verbs, nouns

PROCESSES: Visualising, connecting, improvising

# C7 Mini Men and Women

## Design your own Mini Men and Women

COMMENT: You will be amazed by how much the children enjoy this classic starter. They could model their drawings on the Mr. Men and Little Miss creations of Roger Hargreaves.

**1**

YEAR 5

Mrs Creativity

Mr Creativity

Baby Creativity

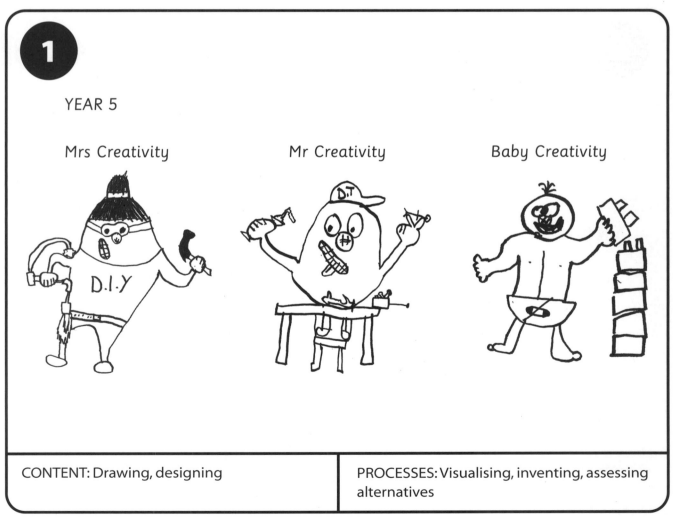

CONTENT: Drawing, designing

PROCESSES: Visualising, inventing, assessing alternatives

# Cartoon Time

## Design your own cartoon character

COMMENT: This is a great starter whenever a cartoon character or storyline makes the news such as on Micky Mouse's 'birthday' or because of a new film. As an extension, children could write a storyline for a cartoon character invented by themselves or others.

**1** YEAR 5

| CONTENT: Cartoons, drawing, designing | PROCESSES: Visualising, comparing, inventing |
|---|---|

C9

# Calligraphy

## Design special capital letters like those often used to start chapters in books

COMMENT: Children love to experiment with letter design. Some chosen sets of letters could be scanned into computers and used as start letters for children's writing.

**1**

YEAR 3

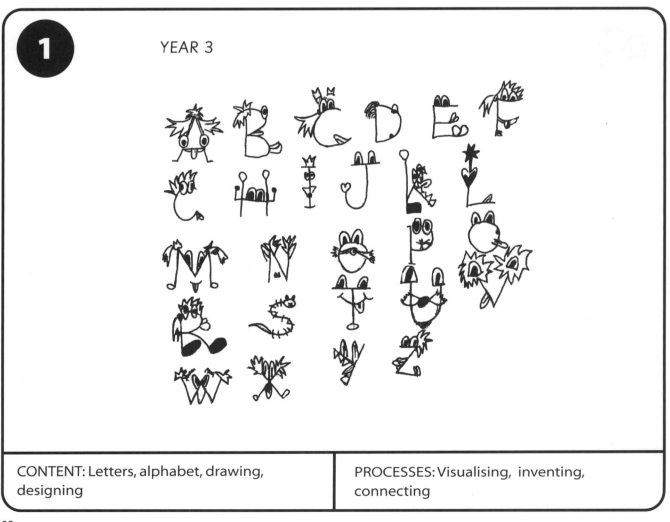

CONTENT: Letters, alphabet, drawing, designing

PROCESSES: Visualising, inventing, connecting

# C10 Photo Time

## What is happening in the photograph?

COMMENT: The power of photography is unique. Put a photograph with no clear meaning up on the board or a picture of someone with an interesting expression. Ask children think about what is happening or what people might be thinking. It is so useful to collect a bank of photographs. A photo linked to a particular area of study could be used to excellent effect. On this page, we have two ideas but no examples. Results will be particular to the photographs you will have at your disposal.

## What are the people saying in this photograph?

COMMENT: Who can create the best or funniest caption to a well chosen photograph?

| CONTENT: Photography | PROCESSES: inventing, improvising, assessing alternatives, connecting |
|---|---|

# C11 Logos

## Design your own logo for an imaginary product

COMMENT: Logos play a very prominent role in society. Children could start by listing ones they know and then design their own. Interesting links to literacy when looking at adverts.

**1**

YEAR 4

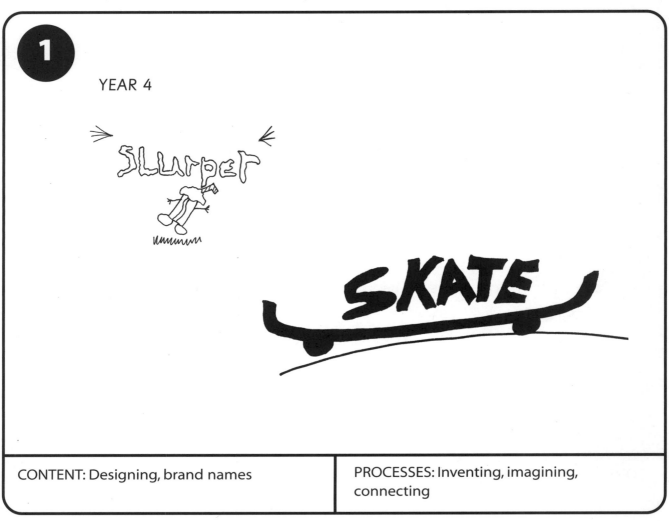

| CONTENT: Designing, brand names | PROCESSES: Inventing, imagining, connecting |
|---|---|

C12

# Flag It Up

## What would the flags of the countries in your new planet look like?

COMMENT: Children love designing new flags. Conventions of flag design may be useful as a guideline i.e. shape, size, colours. This one is closely related to 'On a different planet'.

YEAR 2

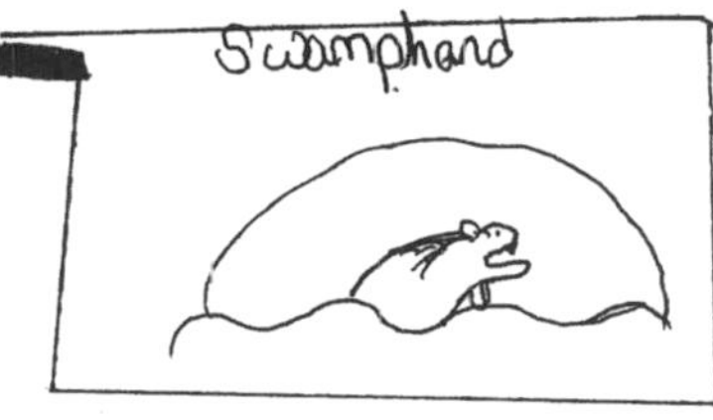


2

YEAR 5

Thinking Land

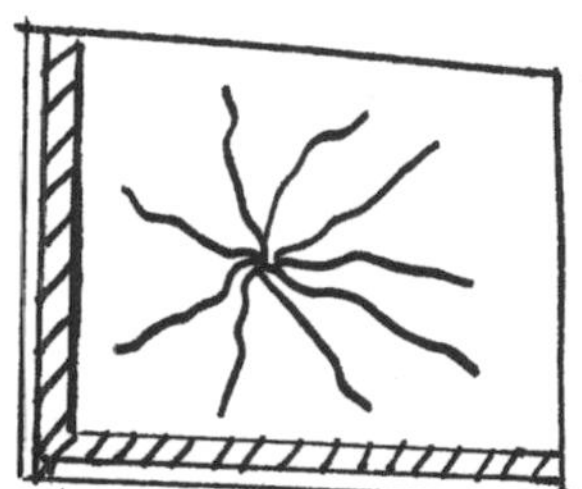

topsy turvy land

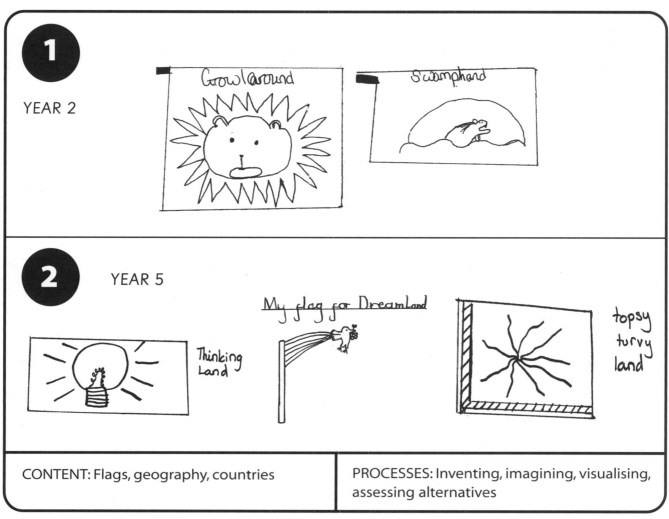

CONTENT: Flags, geography, countries

PROCESSES: Inventing, imagining, visualising, assessing alternatives

# Classics

## How many classic designs can you think of?

COMMENT: The concept of classic design is fascinating. What stands the test of time? The coca-cola bottle for example, or the Eiffel Tower. This can lead to really interesting discussions when children are asked for reasons.

**1**

YEAR 5

| | |
|---|---|
| Coke bottle | Eiffel Tower |
| Guitar | London taxi |
| Rockets | Telephone box |
| Surf boards | Jaguar E-type |
| Light bulb | Picture frames |
| Human body | Wine bottle |

CONTENT: Design and technology

PROCESSES: Valuing, comparing, giving reasons

C14

# Paper Round

## If you were to edit a Newspaper, what sections would you include?

COMMENT: Older children will love the freedom to create something for public consumption. This one ties in very well with aspects of literacy. They could go on to design the front page as an ICT exercise.

**1**

YEAR 6

Film review

General news

Local news

Interviews

Sports

Entertainment

Finance

Issues

Property

Puzzles

Jobs

| CONTENT: Newspapers | PROCESSES: Assessing alternatives, prioritising, imagining |
|---|---|

## C15 Prime Minister

**What changes would you introduce to improve the lives of children, grown ups, retired people?**

COMMENT: This is so good! I am always amazed with how sensible their ideas are! We have on many occasions being tempted to submit them to Parliament!

YEAR 3

| Children | Adults | Retired people |
|---|---|---|
| Adults encouraging children to eat healthily.<br>Help for poor people in Africa all countries.<br>All children should have a proper home.<br>Children to have more places to play. | No smoking, especially around other people.<br>Not to have to work for the whole day.<br>Make towns more peaceful by scrapping cars or having one car per family.<br>More holidays for people at work. | Better links with hospitals.<br>More help for the blind.<br>Free entry to health clubs. |

CONTENT: Parliament, politics, society

PROCESSES: Valuing, assessing alternatives, giving reasons

# Extra Starters

# E1 Legs 

## Things with legs

COMMENT: This is very similar to the 'wheels' exercise, and the children will enjoy thinking about all the different contexts in which we use the word leg, including famous phrases such as 'leg up', 'three legged race', and 'you don't have a leg to stand on'.

**1**

YEAR 1

| | |
|---|---|
| Tables | Lobster |
| Chairs | Races |
| Birds | Dinosours |
| Millipedes | Beer mugs |
| Bears | Football matches |
| Bats | Bookshelf |
| Humans | Cows |
| Octopus | Music stand |
| Dust mites | Trolleys |
| Desk | Scaffolding |
| Spider Crab | Aeroplanes |

**2**

YEAR 5

| | |
|---|---|
| Me | Table |
| Frogs | Stool |
| Spiders | Millipede |
| Centipedes | Ant |
| Caterpillar | Hamster |
| Cow | Rabbit |
| Sheep | Bear |
| Ducks | Crow |
| Chickens | Elephant |
| Lambs | Giraffe |
| Bird | Horse |

CONTENT: Legs, objects

PROCESSES: Connecting, classifying, visualising

E2

# Wheels

## Things with wheels

COMMENT: Encouraging the children to think creatively really pays dividends with this one and a few examples from the list below may be needed to spark their thinking.

**1**

YEAR 1

Unicylce
Car
Bicycle
Roller coaster
Roller skates
Tricycle

**2**

YEAR 6

Tractor
Skater
Hospital bed
Combine harvester
Swirly chains
Legoland cars
Cart
Camper Van
Trike
Penny farthing bike
wheel chair
motor bike
Roller
Skate boards
Unicylce
Cameras
Ferris wheel
London eye

CONTENT: Wheels, objects

PROCESSES: Connecting, classifying, visualising

# E3 Inseparable

## Things that go together!

COMMENT: Once children start this one, they cannot stop! It makes them think so widely and out of the context of school. It can be very funny. When children have compiled their lists, ask them to think about the connections between the items that go together. How are they similar and different? Are they opposites? Can opposites be similar in some ways?

**1**

YEAR 5

Salt and Pepper
On and Off
Up and Down
Fish and Chips
Bread and Butter
Pull and Push
Right and Left
Table and Chair
Pen and Paper
Big and Small
Sun and Moon

Rich and Poor
X and Y
Piglet and Winnie the Pooh
North and South
Please and Thank you
Oranges and Lemons
Plus and Minus
Snow and Ice
Teacher and Voice
Happy and Sad
Cheese and tomato

| CONTENT: Common phrases | PROCESSESS: Making connections, comparing, devising methods |
| --- | --- |

# E4 Our Wonderful World

**Create a list of different countries and as many categories as you can**

COMMENT: This starter is so good at highlighting the human and cultural variety of our world. Ask the children to group the countries into continents or hemispheres. How many other categories for countries can the children think of?

**1**

YEAR 5
Ghana
Zimbabwe
Iraq
Egypt
Switzerland
Australia
China
Sweden
Brazil

**2**

YEAR 5
CATEGORIES
North/south
English speaking
Rich/poor
Continents
Big/small
At war/at peace
Places I'd like to go for my holidays

CONTENT: Countries, languages

PROCESSES: Remembering, classifying, questioning

E5

# Nighty Night

## Who works at night?

COMMENT: I never imagined there were so many! It is interesting to do this one with younger and older children and then compare the two lists. Younger ones often think of examples that older ones miss, and vice versa.

1

YEAR 5

TV people
Pilots
Doctors, surgeons and nurses
Firemen
Policemen
Bar workers
Actors
Security guards
Djs
Bands
Vets
Taxi Drivers
Train Drivers
Burglars

CONTENT: Jobs

PROCESSESS: Devising methods, remembering, classifying

# PMI



## Create a P.M.I. of...

COMMENT: This is one of Edward De Bono's thinking strategies. It's purpose is to stop children jumping to judgements by having them think of about what is interesting about the question, choice or topic to be addressed. What they decide is interesting often transforms their later thinking about what is positive and negative. So, have children list their thoughts about topics under the headings of P (plus) M (minus) and I (interesting). See what happens and be prepared to discuss their lists with them asking for reasons.

YEAR 5: Our philosophy lessons

| PLUS | MINUS | INTERESTING |
|---|---|---|
| We respect each other's points of views | Our minds can't think as deeply as adults | All the issues we discuss |
| Makes lots of connections with the outside world | You feel left out if you have nothing to say | That we do it in school! |
| Makes you a good questioner | You could get into an argument if you really disagree | Children have different ideas to adults |
| There are no limits | You might talk about things which some people have no knowledge of | It can be about anything |
| It makes you think so deeply | | How people take so much for granted |
| | | It leads to other questions |

CONTENT: PMI

PROCESSES: Speculating, imagining, giving reasons, valuing, enquiring

E7

# Odd One Out

**Which is the odd one out and why?**

| Africa | America |
|---|---|
| Australasia | India |

COMMENT: A real classic, never failing to induce the most imaginative thinking. The choice inside the boxes could be anything, related or unrelated to current topics. It also works brilliantly with four numbers. Encourage children to think of more that one possible 'odd one out'. They will have to discuss a range of possible similarities and differences.

**1**

YEAR 5

India, Africa, America, Australasia

India is the odd one out because the rest are continents and it is the only one that starts with an 'I' and that doesn't start and end with an 'a'.

**2**

YEAR 5

Oxygen, Copper, Mercury, Carbon

Oxygen is the odd one out because it is the only gas. Oxygen is the only one that helps us breathe.

CONTENTS: Countries, any curriculum topic

PROCESSES: Classifying, comparing, giving reasons

E8

# The Olympics

## Sports at the Olympics

COMMENT: Sports and disciplines within sports both count. This starter always leads to a discussion about the pros and cons of amateurism vs professionalism, whether professionals should be allowed to take part in the Olympics and whether games like darts should be olympic sports. Ask children to think of as many categories as they can for the sports they have listed. Is there a difference between sports and games?

**1**

YEAR 2
Football
Cricket
Tennis
Pentathlon
Gymnastics
Snooker
Show jumping
Golf
Athletics
Chess

**2**

YEAR 5
CATEGORIES
Ball games
Tiring sports
Mind sports (eg chess)
Games (but not sports)
Sports (but not Olympic sports)
Amateur/professional sports
Track and field

CONTENT: Sport, P.E., games, olympics

PROCESSES: Remembering, classifying, giving reasons

## E9 Very Alphabetical Words 

THINK of words where some or all of the letters in the word are in consecutive alphabetical order.

**First**

COMMENT: This one is very tricky. The children will enjoy seeing which combinations of letters are most common.

**1**

YEAR 3

No
Know
Hi
Mop
Not
Hill
Hit
Not

**2**

YEAR 5

Fabien
Stable
Abby
Jude
Rabbit
Scientists
Kabir
Universe
Abracadabra
Optimistic
Therefore
November
Last
Illustrated
High
Thirst
Saab
Autumn
Dead
Fist
Noticed
Department

CONTENT: Sentence structure, spelling, alphabet

PROCESSES: Devising methods, experimenting and checking

# If Only...

## Who would you like to meet most and why?

COMMENT: This is a chance for children's imaginations to go wild. The people they choose do not have to be famous or real it's completely up to them. This one goes with Dinner Party (P12) and Heroes and Heroines (P15).

**1**

YEAR 4

*Pharaohs: ask them about hieroglyphics.*

*Anthony Horowitz: my favourite author who could inspire me to write about agents.*

*Cara: a friend in Africa, to find out about her life.*

*Doctor Who: to help me travel back in time.*

*My sister: I never got to see her.*

*Nelson Mandela: because I want to tell him how much I appreciate what he has done.*

*Kevin Pieterson: to find out how to become such a good professional sportsperson.*

*My Grandparents who I never got the chance to meet.*

| CONTENT: Famous people, respecting others | PROCESSES: Prioritising, imagining, giving reasons, assessing alternatives |
|---|---|

E11

# Proverbs

## How many proverbs can you think of

COMMENT: This starter is great for PHSME, philosophy, literacy and many other curriculum areas. It will promote discussion on school values. As with 'Lessons in Life' (P18), ask the children to interpret the proverbs and think of examples from real life or stories. Focus on different interpretations to compare and explore the reasons for the differences with children. Ask children to thing of situations where following the advice of the proverb might not be a good idea.

1

YEAR 5

Two wrongs don't make a right.

Don't go crying over spilt milk.

Don't make a mountain out of a molehill.

Don't count your chickens before they hatch.

Sticks and stones may break my bones but names will never hurt me.

Don't judge a book by its cover.

Every cloud has a silver lining.

If you don't have anything nice to say, don't say anything at all.

| CONTENT: Lists, open-ended. proverbs | PROCESSES: Remembering, enquiring, comparing, interpreting |
|---|---|

# Thinking Skills Starters: The Bigger Picture

Towards the end of the last century educationalists, artists and people from the world of business gathered in London for an international arts conference organised by the British Council. One of the speakers, a businessman, complained of the problems he and other company executives had in recruiting the types of employees they needed to move their businesses forward.

He complained that although graduates and school leavers had achieved the relevant qualifications and acquired the basic skills, they lacked creativity, imagination and the ability to innovate. He also went on to criticise teachers for ignoring these crucial aspects of a person's education.

Of course, teachers in the audience responded vehemently both in the question and answer session which followed and in the bar afterwards. Their view – that among teachers can be found some of the most creative, imaginative and innovative people around – was supported by artists who had worked in schools. Many attendees argued that teachers' opportunities to be creative had been stifled by the restrictive nature of the National Curriculum and the Literacy and Numeracy Strategies. Although some delegates were eager to discard the National Curriculum and the Strategies, more were eager to keep them but adapt them to allow more creative teaching and learning.

When the National Curriculum was introduced in 1989, it focused teachers' attentions on what they should be teaching – the content of lessons. The Literacy and Numeracy Strategies turned teachers' attentions to how they should teach. In recent years greater attention has focused on how children learn, with an emphasis on teaching children thinking skills, and on what children learn. There is a growing awareness that the attitudes children develop towards their learning will have a huge impact on their achievements as they progress on their educational journey.

Andy Hargreaves in addressing headteachers in Bristol during their annual conference in March 2004 suggested that we should not return to the 'Julie Andrews' curriculum when teachers walked into classrooms with a few of their favourite things and that we should also move away from the 'Karaoke' curriculum, where teachers follow somebody else's bouncing ball on top of a text beyond their control or influence.

Hargreaves did not go on to say what kind of a curriculum we should be following but perhaps it could be a 'jazz' curriculum where we are all following the same basic riff but with the freedom to pursue our own improvised lines.

In the DfES strategy for primary schools, *Excellence and Enjoyment*, school leaders are encouraged to interpret the National Curriculum and the Strategies flexibly in order to establish the kinds of schools that would best meet the needs of their own pupils. Schools will have to achieve basic literacy and numeracy standards and provide a broad and balanced curriculum – but what else? Many schools, in exploring their vision and mission statements, have looked at the values and attitudes they wish to encourage in their pupils. The phrase 'a positive attitude towards learning' often occurs. The inclusion of *Starters* within a thinking-skills approach to the learning contributes to this positive development.

- *Starters* provide children with opportunities to try new things without being judged. There are no pre-conceived good and bad solutions to *Starters*. Children carry out the first assessment of their own learning.

- *Starters* give children the opportunity to think of creative solutions to problems and to suggest problems that might become future *Starters*. Children can produce many alternative solutions and, if they are not satisfied with their first attempts, they are encouraged to try again.

- Enabling children to be inventive by working on *Starters* will enhance their self esteem. That, in turn, will help them to learn at other times during the week. If children can be more creative in their science, more resilient in their DT and more proficient in making connections in their history then they will become more effective learners, whatever the subject.

- *Starters* develop children's resilience when they stick to a challenge and see it through beyond several attempts.

- Encouraging children to continue working on *Starters* that interest them develops their appetite for questioning, finding out, trying alternative solutions to problems and developing their own personal projects. These dispositions or 'Habits of Mind' are essential attributes of independent learners.

- Sometimes the children have talked about their *Starters* at home and parents have asked teachers and headteachers what is going on in the classrooms. Few other activities have generated so much positive home/school liaison.

In January 2003 David Milliband, in a speech to the Black Country Creative Partnerships, described the kind of education he wanted for children at the beginning of this new century: '...it is vital to get the basics right ... but we also know that a creative curriculum, creative teaching methods, creative use of school time and school staff, creative after-school activities can help young people fulfil their potential. We want all children to master the basic skills, but we also want them to become confident, enthusiastic learners'. Using *Thinking Skills Starters* will not suddenly transform your classrooms into areas of educational excellence but the *Starters* will help you to use time more creatively, will contribute to a more creative curriculum and will provide an enjoyable start to the day for teachers and children.

# The Four Fours Challenge

There are many wonderful things about teaching, but one of the most wonderful of all, I feel, is when a child or group of children present me with one of those very special 'magical moments'.

Using *Starters*, I sometimes experience such moments when children share work with me and the rest of the class which goes far beyond what I was expecting. This was the case when the *Four Fours Challenge* (see page 23) became an obsession with several groups of pupils. The seeds of the magical moments that followed were sown seven years ago, on a wet Tuesday afternoon, half way through my PGCE year at the University of the West of England. Our Maths tutor, Colin Miller, introduced us to the *Four Fours Challenge*. His sessions, I remember, were by far my favourite times on the course, not only because I shared his contagious love of numbers but also because he loved to teach us by going off at tangents – pursuing paths outside the remit of what he should have been covering. His main aim was not to teach us content and process skills but to make us understand the nature of mathematics and the mechanisms behind the concepts which we normally take for granted.

As a pupil in the class that Tuesday afternoon, I remember feeling in my element, as soon as the challenge was explained. The idea is to use 'four fours' and any mathematical operation to make these four fours equal whole numbers.

For example:

$$\frac{4+4}{4+4} = 1$$

Colin set us working by asking us to use four fours each time to try to work out all the numbers from 1 to 20. As soon as we set to work on the challenge, some of us realised that we were getting quite addicted. We were having such fun playing with numbers. Apparently '19' had never been derived before and I remember feeling so proud when I managed to crack it! I knew that one day I wanted the children in my class to experience what I had experienced.

Four years ago, when I arrived at Westbury Park Primary School as a Year 5 teacher, I set the children the *Four Fours Challenge* as one of our *Thinking Skills Starters*. As with the PGCE cohort, I suggested the children try to derive all the numbers from 1 to 20.

The outcome, twenty minutes later was truly extraordinary! Not only were all the children enjoying the challenge, but a small group also had managed to derive all the numbers up to 20. I could not believe it! The enthusiasm of this small group was such that I made *Four Fours* the focus of that week's Maths Investigation Session.

At this stage I realised that, in order for them to start deriving numbers higher than 20, they would need to be introduced to some slightly more complex mathematical operations. I explained to them things like factorials, powers, square roots, brackets and so on.

$4! = 4 \times 3 \times 2 \times 1 = 24$
and $4^0 = 1$
and $4^2 = 16$
and $4^3 = 64$

And they loved it! Children have an amazing ability to soak up information when they regard learning as fun, as playing, as being allowed to do something that is not on the prescribed menu.

That investigation lesson was the beginning of something very special. No sooner had the day finished, than a group of boys decided to get together after school and keep working on the challenge. A few days later they presented me with an immaculately drawn out A1 piece of card containing the answer to all the numbers to 100! Several things amazed and delighted me as I unfolded their poster. I couldn't believe how addicted this group of children had become, and how determined they were to keep challenging themselves to achieve something that had never been done before at school or at the PGCE course. The dedication with which they drew the grid and wrote the numbers, working collaboratively, surpassed all expectations and went beyond anything they had ever done in class. The poster immediately became the subject of conversation amongst the rest of the school and they took the customary walk down the corridor to show Alan Rees, our headteacher.

*Once we started I was hooked. I enjoyed the hardest the most (93 to 97). It was great working them out with my friends* (Beanie). *When it got harder, it was more enjoyable because the challenge was bigger* (Jim). *Making so many numbers using different methods, like factorials and powers was what we enjoyed the most. We are now using all these techniques in secondary school and we feel we have a head start! It helped us develop teamwork, patience, determination and the skill of working with other people* (Xander, Jim, Beanie).

A year later, still teaching Year 5, I tried it all again. I introduced my pupils to the story as it had developed up until then and set them working. Again the addiction bug bit and this time it was Michael and Lewis who set out to equal and surpass the '100' mark. This they did magnificently and through sheer resilience. They eventually reached up to '150' and went on to present it in an equally wonderful wall chart. These charts have become permanent fixtures in my classroom and intimate companions at all presentations to other teachers.

*It was hard at first but Michael helped me along and, when Michael got stuck, I helped him and we decided to work together. I liked the fact that this type of maths investigation was a different sort of challenge. Working without help gave us a lot of independence. I liked the fact that it was hard and challenging. It was frustrating when we got stuck on a number and it took ages to work it out but we had a sense of triumph when we managed to crack it. It's made me more confident now in secondary school. It helped me with my knowledge of maths in general and it helped me to stick at problems. I felt special and valued. It helped me to work with other people and share ideas* (Lewis).

*Michael that night discussed it with his mathematically inclined father and started working at 9pm and just carried on. Two years later, aged 12, he is up to 550, more than his brother Joe, but Joe doesn't know! Michael became more confident and cheerful through doing the challenge* (Parent of Michael H)

Nothing, however, could have prepared me for what was to happen this term. This year the class contains Will and Joe H, brothers of Lewis and Michael respectively, the partnership that reached '150'. They also adore numbers and took on the challenge with tremendous enthusiasm. The buzz from the whole year group in the maths investigation session just before the end of Term One had to be seen to be believed. The two brothers were soon joined by four more friends and they managed to derive all the numbers up to '200'. Their devotion extending to play times, dinner times and after-school times.

*When we were first told about it, it sounded exciting and interesting and just the sort of thing I like doing. We carried on in Golden Time (their precious free time) because it was so interesting. I had to concentrate and be resilient. I liked working with my friends, helping each other. 115 sticks out in my mind because Kabir had an idea and Joe put it together to get a number, and at break time, we just couldn't stop thinking about it* (Will).

*I remember my brother doing this and I just wanted to start it. I got hooked straight away and I wanted to do more than my brother. My confidence has really improved* (Joe).

This morning, the day after the half-term break, Joe, after spending the week's holiday working on the challenge, presented me with every number up to '522', and he is still going! I could not believe what I was seeing and it took me a while to react; I was in total shock!

*Joe wanted to do more than his brother had done and enjoyed doing the challenge at school with his two best friends and Alex and Luna, but over half term he got up to 522. His confidence has increased and he is very pleased that in this area of mathematics he can do as well as his brother. Sibling rivalry is alive and well in the Healy household. It has had quite a positive effect on them both* (Parent of Joe).

I have no idea if, when and how this story will develop. I said to the children that it may be that there are numbers which may be impossible to do, but I think this has only prompted them to want to keep going even more. It is a truly outstanding story that to me sums up the very best of Primary Education. The open-ended, investigative approach to learning, the dispositions of mind that these children are developing, the immeasurable benefits to their self esteem, their willingness to keep going, their resilience and lack of worry when dealing with something that at first seems like an impossible task, their pattern-seeking and spotting, and their willingness to feel free to play with numbers are all the things that I think make teaching so worthwhile and rewarding.

*The Four Fours Challenge is a great way of thinking and it is very addictive* (Chris). *I love all of it but particularly that it's all about exploring and investigating different methods of playing with numbers and you can go on and on. I've developed a deeper understanding in investigative maths* (Luna).

*When you finish a number you feel great and that you've really achieved something. I like doing them in my head and on post-it notes. It's given me a lot of confidence* (Alex).

Although the *Four Fours Challenge* is an extreme example, very similar levels of enthusiasm have emerged as a result of starting everyday with a *Thinking Skills Starter*. This, we feel, is providing us with a model of how children and adults can become 'responsible individuals who take great pleasure in learning' (our school's mission statement).

# Index

*Showing Starter number and page number.*